A SMALL DIFFERENCE

A SMALL DIFFERENCE

RAYMOND PLANK

Founder, Apache Corporation

 **VANTAGE**Press

NEW YORK

Cover and interior design by Molly M. Black

Vantage Press and the Vantage Press colophon
are registered trademarks of Vantage Press, Inc.

FIRST EDITION

Published by Vantage Press, Inc.
419 Park Ave. South, New York, NY 10016

Manufactured in the United States of America
ISBN: 978-0-533-16526-1
Library of Congress Catalog Card No. on file.

0 9 8 7 6 5 4 3 2 1

CONTENTS

INTRODUCTION

THE CAPACITY OF THE HUMAN mind for learning and personal growth greatly exceeds that which I would have deemed plausible in my early years. The purpose of this memoir is to open the window on my life in the hope that readers may find parts useful in achieving a fuller measure of their own capacities to attain worthy goals on behalf of self and others—in the certain belief that happiness and understanding uplift the human spirit, contributing to the base for a full and happy life.

I look back through the years of my life from the vantage point of now being in my ninetieth year. I look back in order to see forward. Hindsight informed me of several primary individual life-time learnings which might be useful to others, especially those who desire to expand the remarkable individual capacities granted us when we seek beyond self the greater common good.

My values have been influenced by three cornerstones.

First, at perhaps the age of ten, when I was on a walk with my dad, he dropped my hand, put his arm around my shoulder, and noted, "Son, over my life I've found it useful to try to make a very small difference on behalf of others." He obviously preferred that I mull this comment, for he was not open for questions from his ten-year-old child. He concluded with, "Mother will be calling us to dinner; time to get back." We never again discussed the topic, still fresh and oft recurring in my mind now, nearly eighty years later.

The second major impact was that of a penny postcard my mother had written just prior to her death at age forty-seven, when I was fifteen:

> My Son,
> The fifteen years of my life which you have shared have been such glorious ones. How I have loved them. You are so fine and unselfish. You have given me such love and consideration. I have known no joy which could equal that of your companionship. My pride in you will go on through the years if you keep your head up and your courage and faith high.
> All Love,
> Mother

Mother died of a blood clot to the brain following a routine appendectomy, only hours before I was to drive my father to the hospital and bring her home.

The third major cornerstone was the death and disablement of many friends and acquaintances in World War II. Had they died in vain? Would it be a better world? Did I have a responsibility to them? Why was I spared unscathed after forty combat missions in the Pacific theater? Between 1938 and 1946, war was to us, inevitable. It dominated our thought, training, education, and activities for eight years.

With the clarity of hindsight, I see that the three cornerstones had much to do with the career path I pursued. I chose to be self-employed, rather than work for a larger company, because I wanted my platform for growth and outreach to be in business rather than public service, politics, or the ministry, the three alternatives I considered. Having chosen business, I needed to decide whether my career would be in a large, stable company or a small, riskier initiative. Having considered the larger established business options during World War II well before surviving it, I set my course within two months of my return from combat on the smaller enterprise.

This memoir is not traditionally dedicated, for were it to be, the list of those both loved and respected would be so long it would require multiple volumes for specific dedications to cover them. Nor does it cite multiple personal acknowledgements in the hundreds to identify, include, or omit those important to my life and shared values into my ninetieth year. Rather, I would recognize those I do not here name with my spirit, hope, and soul, and encourage them to pursue lifetime learning. It's not about what we get; it's about how we get it and how we use it. I've known many youths with a strong work ethic and integrity, who have been highly successful; so many school teachers who have inspired me—they are giants among us. It isn't what we inherit or pursue, it's about whether and how we elect to grow.

Apache Corporation had a very modest beginning, founded as a public company with $250,000 in 1954 by Truman Anderson, Charles "Chuck" Arnao, and myself. By mid-2008, that $250,000 had become $50 billion. Stock and share splits brought down the original share cost from $10.00 to 4¢ per share; the share price reached $147 in mid-2008, my last full year with Apache as its chairman. The shares, which then numbered 335 million, paid 60¢ per year in dividends, fifteen times the 4¢ per share adjusted initial price. The annual dividends equaled $201 million,

804 times the initial investment.

When I left Apache in 2009, one of the corporation's senior exploration managers, Rob Johnston, wrote me the following letter:

> Mr. Plank, how can one measure the trickle-down value to humanity of a successful company? How many past, present and future generations of Apache families, contractors, mineral owners and others have or will have raised and educated children, married sons and daughters and supported aged parents and grandparents partly by the wealth created by you and Apache? How many teachers or students will someday change the world? It has been said that every person on earth is only six steps away from contact with every other person. In your case, I believe the degree of separation is much closer.

Teddy Roosevelt, once opined, "Better to have lived one hour of glorious strife, than never to have lived at all."

You be the judge. Let the tale begin.

Hand in hand with my dad.

EARLY YEARS

MY LIFE BEGAN MAY 29, 1922, in Eitel Hospital in Minneapolis, Minnesota. As the last of four children, I was soon destined, like my siblings and both parents, to be redheaded, and in the summer, freckled.

My father, Raby Plank, had preceded my birth by fifty-seven years, in Huntington Township, Pennsylvania, July 1865. Two years earlier in 1863, the armies of the North and of the South had plundered the area around Gettysburg, as America's Civil War raged and ravaged North and South. A number of Plank family farmers had done quite well until their fences were torn down, their livestock driven off to feed the soldiers who fought long and hard and died in the area. My father, to supplement the family's struggle for economic survival, worked both on the farm and in the coal mine, three times succumbing to pneumonia. Then, with $25, a princely sum in 1882, he followed his older brother, my uncle Will, to Minneapolis.

By the time he arrived, the socio-economic power structure of Minnesota had already been cast—a consideration of little or no interest to my father, or to me, then or now. The "upper crust" was largely concentrated within a small radius on high ground overlooking downtown Minneapolis. Close by were cultural institutions such as the Walker Art Center and the Minneapolis Art Institute, and perhaps fifty years later, the Guthrie Theater with its focus on drama. Across the Mississippi on the St. Paul side grew the land grant University of Minnesota, home of the symphony orchestra, conducted in my early years by Eugene Ormandy. The Minnesota social circles of the "city fathers" and theirs were narrowly exclusive, particularly in their country clubs.

The churches at which this social elite worshipped, while few, were well attended, while the art-based institutions appealed to a far wider population base, to which the cultural attributes were a great asset. The arts were strongly supported by both individuals and the city business base, which grew rapidly in both Minneapolis and its "twin city across the river," St. Paul. Class differences were more apparent within the marriage patterns of the generations at the time, which carried over to the private schools attended, and to the executive positions with the two major banks, Northwestern National and First National. The award for excellence should go to the city's fathers for their planning, foresight, and effort to achieve excellence in the outreach from public schools in their commitments of time, toward achieving a quality of life for all. The power base cared and shared, and the quality of life in present-day Minneapolis shows it, matching the beauty and topography of "the City of Lakes" and its amenities. It was and is a vibrant environment, friendly to the upward mobility of its citizens from which I benefited greatly.

I used to quip that I was born on one side of the tracks, but I grew up on both sides and appreciated both.

The closest Dad came to the negative side of the social pecking

With my Mother, in 1922.

order was in his comment, "Lots of folks seem to get lost trying to keep up with the Joneses, where their efforts could better be applied elsewhere."

I find it useful to recognize that lifetime learning and education are the cornerstones of full and happy lives; while working values, integrity, strong work, and saving ethics are both the mortar and building blocks upon which to build, in the words of Glenn Miller, one's individual "stairway to the stars . . . out yonder where the blue begins."

My mother, Maud Ruth Howe, was also born in a farming community, in Redfield, South Dakota, in 1897. Mother was the "educated" parent, having graduated from high school before moving to Minneapolis at age eighteen in 1915. Dad had dropped out after seventh grade. When she met my father in Minneapolis, she was attending Northwest Bible School. She

My family just before my arrival: my brother Raby (who died at six), Mother and Dad, Becky, and Ruth.

continued the learning process through self-instruction. No doubt my parents' limited education loomed large in their commitment to the best education possible for their children.

Religion was a common denominator on both sides of the family and significantly influenced the upbringing of my two older sisters, Ruth and Rebecca, or Becky, as she was known to all. Both names were biblical, as was all our upbringing, which was harder on my sisters, twelve and ten years older than me, respectively. Dancing and parties were not on their social agenda, and even the tame small-screen black-and-white movies were frowned upon. Music was limited to large, wax recordings manually changed.

Minneapolis, on the banks of the Mississippi, was small, young, and vibrant. The economy of Minneapolis was as robust as western Pennsylvania was bereft of opportunities. Timber and iron ore from northern Minnesota were complemented by wheat and corn from the west and south of the state. Real estate was rapidly developing. River transportation and shipments of iron ore to the steel mills down the Great Lakes to Chicago, Cleveland, and Pittsburgh made Minneapolis the gateway to the west, served by the network of railroads, with linkage by water and rail to Chicago and New Orleans. Wheat was milled to flour both in Minnesota and as far east as Buffalo, New York.

My father had no trouble finding his first job as a bookkeeper. (Many years later, this was to be my first business career as well, and though I had gone to night school after taking correspondence courses in the South Pacific during World War II, my accounting and tax background had more holes than Swiss cheese. My college major was international relations, and the only course I dropped at Yale was economics.) After stints at bookkeeping and selling paper, Dad entered the printing business, eventually becoming president and controlling shareholder of Harrison and Smith Printing Company, "Good Printers Since 1871." Good printers they were, serving a number of the area's growing regional and national businesses. My father had started as a salesman. Dad was honest, friendly, bright, open, and motivated. He also had a great sense of humor.

Until I entered the first grade, I had spent my years virtually alone with my parents. My older brother, named Raby for Dad, had died at age six of scarlet fever. This was an era prior to miracle drugs such as the Salk vaccine against polio. My mother sought to restrict my exposure to all forms of communicable diseases and I did not fully warm to social isolation. Their concerns about my health contributed to my parents' acquiring 80 acres and building a home in the countryside, which they believed was a sufficient barrier from the germs of Minneapolis.

My sisters' activities were largely home centered: learning

Pulling a wagon, 1924.

to sew, knit, and helping our mother with housework while involved in school, Sunday school, church services, visiting friends' houses, and picnics. Occasionally, a boat ride on nearby Lake Minnetonka brightened their days.

It was better, I thought, to be a boy brought up in the country than in the city—for, in both warm summers and cold winters, I lived out of doors. The yard and its trees were home to squirrels, rabbits, orioles, cardinals, blue jays, blackbirds, doves, frogs, and their commingled sounds of life and joy. But my limited contact with children of my own age made me a fish out of water when later I found myself surrounded by hundreds of children at Wayzata Public School. There, I was totally impervious to reading instruction. Soon I was transferred to Blake School in Minneapolis and the tutorial skills of Miss MacDonald, my first grade teacher. I used to take eggs to school for her; and her charm, and possibly enriched diet, brought me up to speed within weeks.

As soon as I began to write, I started to scratch out a daily diary that the superb Miss MacDonald told me would help my

Attending the Harrison & Smith Co. picnic.

wayward penmanship and sentence structure. My diary writing has continued for eighty more years and has proved its value.

Another lifelong habit began in my childhood. Dad had given me a coin bank in the form of a copper Liberty Bell. When Dad thought I had enough coins to open a savings account, he announced we were going to take my Liberty Bell bank to the First National Bank and open a savings account. Until we made our trip together, I had thought the bank would be shaped like my smaller Liberty Bell.

I was not allowed to swim either in Lake Minnetonka or in any of the Minneapolis lakes. Lake Minnetonka received the lawn fertilizer and sewage from many of the summer houses along its shores. I did not learn to swim until I went to Yale University, where it was required. Instead I was loading hay onto the wagon and into our two hay barns, while later reading books about Horatio Alger and everything Zane Grey wrote of the west, keeping Mother's library card, and eventually my own, busy.

I may have lived an isolated life, but there were immense compensations for an action-oriented boy with unrestricted ac-

Plankheim—our name for home.

cess to outdoor life. I could walk or ride my bike to Plankheim (our name for home), play cops and robbers, and shoot rubber guns, later supplanted by BB guns. In the snowy winters we could sled, toboggan, and dig snow caves in long drifts, sometimes creating several rooms fitted with old blankets on the floor and wooden boxes for stools and tables.

My parents were very religious—prayers at meals and after I climbed into my bed, which was covered by a red and black blanket knitted by Dad's mother in 1856. Sunday was never a working day, "the seventh day of rest," and I attended Sunday school, followed by the full church service. Church failed to hold my interest. The wooden bench seats cut off the circulation in my young legs and I squirmed. I didn't know what the preachers were talking about most of the time. Sunday school wasn't much better, at least not after a small ruffian bashed me on the nose when I told him he should stop stealing pennies from the offering plate. I ran the six blocks home, crying to my parents, my nose bleeding. While Mother cleaned me up, Dad suggested it was time to learn to fight.

Chickens were the beginning.

For me, farm life and responsibilities were also the outcropping of family values and a strong work ethic. Life was structured, and privileges were earned rather than assumed, conferred, or casually granted.

My parents, by ensuing standards—or lack thereof—were strict, but within a structure where absolute truth and integrity were required and good performance praised. I was rewarded with progressively increased opportunity, freedom, and responsibility.

Early on I had chores, which included collecting, cleaning, and keeping track of dozens of eggs for family consumption and sale. As I grew older and more proficient, the egg money became mine, and selling eggs, followed by broilers, gave me some early marketing and sales experience. How fortunate I was to grow up in the country and comprehend self-sufficiency and innovation as building blocks toward independence, broadening my opportunities and confidence.

Chickens were the beginning, followed by digging worms and catching frogs for fisherman at boat providers along Lake Minnetonka, making and selling cider from apples from our or-

My sons Roger and Mike continuing the Plank maple syrup tradition.

chard, and making maple syrup. By high school, I was busy saw-ing down trees (no power saws then), stacking, selling, and stor-ing firewood with which to boil down maple sap to syrup. By late February, maple sap began to run in the trees when the daytime temperature rose above freezing. My boyhood friend, Chuck Arnao, and I whittled sumac about an inch in diameter, eight inches in length. We hollowed out the soft cores and pounded the tapered ends carefully into the holes we had drilled into the maple trunks. This directed the sap to drip into the buckets. We boiled down the sap in pans over wood fires until about 29 gal-lons became a gallon of syrup. This we sold to friends and local grocery stores, while our poultry went to many meat markets and restaurants in Minneapolis, as well as to a list of parents wanting tender, young roosters for home consumption.

For several years when Chuck and I were generating serious money, we had a joint checking account from the chicken and syr-up sales. We used the funds to buy shotguns and ammunition.

I was grounded in Dad's values of integrity, a strong work

Blake School friends—Pete Dorsey & Phil Duff.

ethic, and the desire to be successful. His mentoring was laced with analogies that conveyed a lasting learning base for me. His rules were simple. "Look all people in the eye when you or they speak; never, ever tell me a falsehood; when I request that you do something, it's an order—do it now." With that for structure, we got along just fine. He praised how I cut the lawn and did chores, and was enthusiastic over my budding entrepreneurial endeavors.

Dad may have ended his formal education after the seventh grade, but he certainly was a fine teacher. Often during summer vacation he would walk around the yard with me after a game of croquet and inspect whether I'd picked up the weeds from the garden, or missed patches of grass while pushing the old reel lawnmower. He was particularly interested in whether the tools had been put away; "Everything has its place," he said. Dad was invariably complimentary when the tools, rather than left

11

out to rust or get lost, were back to allotted and marked spaces in the oversized two-car garage with benches and a peg board for tools. "You know, son," he would say, "It always amazes me how tools have a way of walking off."

In 1932, when I was ten, my father and I sat before our single, crackling radio in the dining room listening to commentators on the Tuesday election prognostications on the race between Republican president Hoover and Democrat aspirant Franklin Delano Roosevelt.

The crash of the stock market in 1929 had given rise to massive unemployment and rising fears among Americans. Hoover was depicted as a "do-nothing president," and the voters were ready for change. Roosevelt swept into office, and although he quickly proclaimed a national bank holiday to halt the run on the banks and introduced many initiatives under the New Deal, the U.S. economy did not recover until World War II created a postwar surge from deferred demand.

During the '30s, factories closed, home and farm owners defaulted on mortgages, and families across the nation lost everything. Bread lines and soup kitchens sprang up, people went cold and hungry. Anger and frustration were accompanied by strikes, marches, and hopelessness. Despite the National Recovery Act, the Works Project Administration, and a farm program under Henry Wallace (FDR's secretary of agriculture), under which cattle, sheep, and hogs were slaughtered to raise prices, collective changes did not suffice to turn the economy around.

Nor did my family escape the Great Depression. I recall Dad coming home from the office one night and announcing that his net worth, largely in stocks and bonds, had been wiped out. Yet we had food, much of which we raised, clothing, and a mortgage-free home. There were times when Dad personally had to borrow funds from the First National Bank of Minneapolis to meet the Harrison and Smith payroll. He was fortunate to have credit and credibility as an honest, able businessman, and fortunate the bank was solid enough to have money to lend him.

Dad was scrupulous in paying his bills, and was able to keep me in Blake. Yet on Christmas Day, 1932, when Mother and Dad gave me a Lionel electric train, I cried, because I did not think they could afford it. But the train, and my parents gathering with me before it during winter evenings, in front of a large wood fireplace, became a principal delight.

With my mother.

AFTER MOTHER, LONNIE

ONE NEVER FORGETS THE DEATH of a parent. Mother had gone to the hospital for a routine appendectomy in July 1937. I was to drive Dad to the hospital the Saturday morning, when we would pick her up and return her home. Dad never learned to drive. At three a.m. I was awakened by the phone. A female voice said, "May I speak to Mr. Plank? This is Northwestern Hospital calling." Filled with apprehension, I called Dad, asleep in the master bedroom above me. As he hastened to the phone, I retreated from the dining room to the hallway, and heard my father exclaim, "Oh, no!" Mother was dead at forty-seven, from a blood clot that exercise and blood thinners could have prevented.

As noted earlier, from her hospital bed mother had penciled a note to me on a penny postcard. On her deathbed she also left cards to my father and sisters none of which we shared, respecting each others' privacy.

My sister Ruth had been home from New York for a few days' paid vacation; together we were in shock. Becky and Ruth (nicknamed Ruttie) had long left the nest, Beck to sail with my

My sister Ruth ("Ruttie") and me.

mother to Southampton, England, and then to Cape Town, South Africa, where she married her geologist and mining engineer fiancé, Bill Pettijohn. They made their home in Mufilira, Northern Rhodesia, where Bill, a great guy, became mine manager for a major British mining company. They went on to have two children, an older daughter, Julia, and a son, Tom.

Ruttie, twelve years my senior, had graduated from Milwaukee Downer, and after a sales job at St. Paul's Field Schlick Department Store, moved to Los Angeles and the May Company, from which she joined Wildrick & Miller, an advertising agency in New York City. There she handled the account of one of the first blue denim clothing manufacturers. I was proud of both my red-haired sisters. Ruth was quiet, whimsical, bright and attractive, while Becky was vivacious and outgoing, with a penchant for snaring her older sister's boyfriends.

Later on the morning of my Mother's death, the house filled with my parents' friends, one of whom was a widow, Margie Dameron. She was helpful to Dad in making funeral arrangements, but Ruth and I could hardly stand her wailing and moaning around the house. We needed quiet to move beyond shock. Ruth took a leave of absence from her job and remained home to manage the place, and a bit too much of our lives. Five years later, Dad and Margie would marry.

When I was fourteen, Mother had thought I should begin to see girls. My life in the country and numerous enterprises coupled with Blake's being a boys' country day school rendered girls a rarity in my life, until I met the glorious Lonnie Hoke. For me it was a new and strange yearning, "love at first sight," for Lonnie was a wonderful person. Things were different way back then—"nice" girls and boys waited. In the vacuum created by Mother's death and my sisters' moving on, from when I was fifteen through eighteen, Lonnie was more than a girlfriend. In a way she had replaced all three and was my first love. During the months that followed, Lonnie helped me get beyond the chasm. For six months, I was unable to write in my diary. Lonnie, totally sensitive to the shock, was there for me.

I also filled my life with chickens, and driving too fast with Lonnie. I read volumes of books with my head on my great Doberman, who seemed to sense my bereavement. With Lonnie I questioned, "Why, God?" and "Do you really exist?"

One night as we were driving together Lonnie said, "Pull over here; we need to talk." As we drove off the dirt road into our secluded retreat Lonnie asked, "Raymond, do you believe in God?"

Lonnie Hoke.

As tears streamed down my cheeks I replied, "I used to, but now I question my belief and rather doubt that I do. God is supposed to be just and loving. It doesn't fit. Do you believe in God, Lonnie?"

"Yes, I do," she answered, "I have to."

I continued my query, "Do you believe in life after death, heaven and hell?"

Lonnie answered, "Yes, I believe in the whole country mile, and faith is helpful to me as I hope it may be to you. Prayer can help."

En route to her house I steered with my left knee, we held each other close.

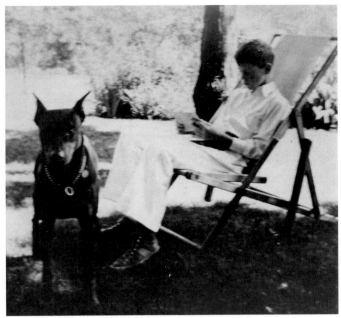

Reading with my Doberman, Von.

A year later, Lonnie would again be supportive. My father had decided we would go on a rare summer vacation. Together with one of Dad's star salesmen, Ed White, we drove east through Civil War battlefields I'd seen previously when visiting Pennsylvania relatives, then to Hershey, Pennsylvania, and the city's chocolate factory. In Washington, D.C., we viewed the U.S. Printing Office; then continued on to New York City, down the coast into Georgia, Tennessee, and Alabama; and then to New Orleans, where we dined at the famous Antoine's. I ordered fish en papillote. Finding it delicious, I complimented the French waiter with the enthusiasm of a sixteen-year-old hick from Minnesota. His response: "But monsieur, you are eating ze paper bag." I felt the embarrassment crawl up my back to my neck and could have slid under the table.

Little did we know what awaited us as we neared New Iberia, Louisiana, the next morning. It was raining lightly as I drove on the two-lane asphalt highway in light traffic. An oncoming car with headlights on pulled out to pass, went into a skid, and hit us head on, even though I had driven the La Salle over halfway onto the shoulder of the road.

There were no seat belts in those days. The impact caused me to hit the steering wheel, slash my chin, break off a tooth, and break my jaw. Glass slashed my right wrist, as a scar still attests. Ed White struck the windshield from the right front seat and laid his scalp open. Dad, seated behind him, pitched forward into Ed, breaking ribs and his collarbone. Both suffered internal injuries; Ed passed out. I was able to force open the driver's door, wobble around and help free Dad from the rear right seat of the car. The ambulance took us to New Iberia Hospital. Ed, requiring more intensive care, was moved to New Orleans. It was months before he reached home, and nearly a year before he returned to Harrison and Smith.

In about a week, Dad was able to travel back to Minneapolis with me by train, bringing a full-time nurse who spent the rest of the summer in Wayzata. Dad went back to work while I had my jaw rebroken and reset, and a new tooth and bridge put in. My jaw was wired shut from July until school started after Labor Day. Lonnie filled my days and evenings with chocolate malts and broth (the only things I could comfortably eat) from the drugstore and tended me with compassion.

The driver of the other car, an inebriated salesman of the Standard Coffee Company of New Orleans, who was driving at a speed not warranted on a wet highway, sustained minor injuries. Both vehicles were totaled. The insurance company sold Dad's new LaSalle for $75. The car was replaced, our medical costs covered, and $20,000 awarded to Dad. Ed White, suffer-

The Plank family LaSalle.

ing a reduction in quality of life and enduring a twelve-month recovery period, received $60,000. But that was an era before the trial lawyers achieved prominence and outsized verdicts.

A formal portrait, 1938.

BLAKE YEARS

MOST OF MY BLAKE CLASSMATES lived in Minneapolis, and when school moved from Blake downtown to the Hopkins campus "senior school," they took the streetcar to the edge of the Blake campus. Three members of my class, Dick Confer, Chuck Arnao, Bill Frankfurter, and I were carpooled by our moms in the mornings to school, arriving before eight fifteen chapel that began each day with a prayer, a hymn, announcements, and, several days per week, with a five-minute talk by an upperclassman speaking before the school and faculty. Initially terrified as a junior, by my senior year, thanks to my debating team practice, I began to feel at ease, developing a style and subject flow that has served me well. It all began in the Blake chapel in 1939.

While attending confirmation class at Westminster Presbyterian Church learning was presided over by Dr. Lowe, a warm and kindly minister, who opened class with a statement, "God is a spirit." Unable to contain myself, I inquired, "What is a spirit, sort of like a ghost?" I don't recall his response, but decades later wondered whether spirituality, and thereby God, were a

Charlie Mead, Phil Duff, and others.

presence inside oneself and whether perhaps when one prayed one was in dialogue within one's self versus "up" or "out there."

Mother had allowed me to play football on the C team, but she benched me before I could go out for the B or A team, preliminary to the varsity. She feared for my well-being, a carryover from her loss of Raby, and in a way, looking back, I can't blame her. My nose, for which helmets of the time provided no protection, bled almost daily over my sweatshirt and pants. Each weekend, Mother laundered my bloody equipment in her ancient Maytag washer and hung it out to dry. My football days were drying up along with my togs.

After Mother passed away, I told my father I really wanted to go out for the varsity football team. He approved of my love of hunting, active physical farm life, and understood my wanting to be a "man's man." The auto accident quashed my junior-year football aspirations. That fall, I was not going to be joining football practice and going out for the varsity—not with my face wired up and my body becoming skinnier by the week. That would wait until my senior year. Instead, Arnao and I sold the late summer

With my father in downtown Minneapolis.

cider to the practicing varsity—until, one hot August afternoon, they came down with diarrhea and our Blake market vanished.

There's no question that my youthful entrepreneurship, coupled with avid hunting, got in the way of scholastic achievement. In some classes I did well; in others, poorly. Was it good teachers versus not so good? Perhaps to a large degree, for in the classes in which I did well, such as English, geography, German, and history, my teachers were superb and shaped my interest and learning. They had a lot to compete with, for if they could not hold my interest, my mind was off and away to the activities and work that did hold my attention.

I'm not sure how I got a passing grade of 60 in Charles Lamb's Latin class, which kept me from the honor roll. What I do know is that I was Lamb's favorite whipping boy and pissing post. Dressed daily in his brown, rumpled sports jacket, gray flannel pants, and bow tie, he had seated me in the front left seat on the aisle, my limbs and body accessible. I would study my next day's Latin assignment until I had it cold. Unfortunately, Lamb would raise his voice and splutter, "And now, class, I'm going to call on Plank. If you'll note closely, you'll see instead of a brain, a malted milk swirling around." I would go blank and the physical harassment would ensue. His tricks included throwing blackboard erasers at me at point-blank range and rapping my fingers with his three-cornered wooden twelve-inch ruler.

Then, one day, he expired of a heart attack.

On the day of his funeral, the flag was lowered to half-mast and school was dismissed after lunch to enable the student body to attend his funeral services. I went to the head of the school, Mr. Alder (nicknamed "the bunny" for his white moustache), and said, "Sir, I don't want to attend Mr. Lamb's funeral and request being excused." His response was, "I believe I understand, and you need not be present."

Fortunately, of all the teachers I've known over the decades, Charlie Lamb was the rankest of the rank, in vivid contrast to the many who were outstanding. The next summer, Lamb's senior in all respects, Noah Foss, called me in for tutoring twice a week, to which I took like a duck to water. Thriving under his mentoring and teaching, my grades shot up. Second-year Latin was one of the courses in which I took honors on my college boards.

Who among us does not have one or a number of teachers we recall vividly, hold in high lifetime regard, and who made a meaningful difference in our early years, contributing to a lifetime of learning and respect?

Although Noah Foss made a dramatic difference in my life, so did a number of others; Miss MacDonald, first grade, both Miss and Mrs. Russell in third and fourth grades; Miss Hauser in fifth and many other great teachers, including Mike Horn, Bill Glenn, and Prescott Cleveland—all fine people who taught warmly and well and followed the lives of "their boys" through World War II and beyond.

"BRIGHT COLLEGE YEARS"
AND THE OUTBREAK OF WAR

DURING THE SUMMER OF 1940, I called a girl I wanted to get to know, Sally Stevens; Sally was a tall, attractive brunette with friendly compassion. She was smart, loved the outdoors, and was graciously absent any tinge of condescension.

Early one morning I received a telephone call from her father, Nathaniel Stevens. He was concerned with my fast driving and scrapes with the local policeman, "Corny" Cornelius, our police chief and my friend with whom I occasionally rode on a few Saturday nights. "Corny" wanted me to witness the blood and agonies of fast driving accompanied by alcohol, which I did not use. I told Sal's father that if allowed to date her, I would be particularly careful and concluded with the comment that I recognized his concern and wanted to compliment him for it. Sally in turn noted her dad was all smiles and commented on what a fine young man I was.

My memory of our first date is limited to a single recollection. We stopped at a White Castle, bought six hamburgers for 25¢ and buttered popcorn for a dime a box, and devoured them before a movie.

Brook Fields, Abe Sheldon, Bud Howe, Ken Dayton, and me at Yale in New Haven.

In September 1940, six of us from Blake and two from its counterpart school, St. Paul Academy, boarded trains to Chicago, and made our way to New York City. From Grand Central Station we transferred to the Hartford and New Haven Line and alighted several hours later in New Haven, Connecticut, to attend Yale.

Not having been north of New York City, I found everything new and very different. Freshmen were housed on the "old campus" in a series of historic buildings with names such as Welsh and Bingham Hall (in which Albert "Abe" Sheldon and I were roommates). On a rainy Sunday afternoon we assembled to be greeted by Yale's president, Charles Seymour, in Battelle Chapel. Seymour dwelled briefly on Yale, turning quickly to the world soon to be engulfed in World War II.

"America is going to war. Look to your right at the face of the man seated next to you. Now look to your left. There is a

In front of Pierson College, Yale.

Throwing a snowball at my friend Ken Dayton during our Western trip.

strong probability that one of you will not return alive."

No one tittered, though it didn't take long for the men of Yale to figure out that with everyone on right and left subject to the dismal outlook, each and all had been embraced by his prediction, except those on the aisle. Although the day was wet and dark, the war clouds dismal, I've often wondered why he spoke as he did. We had been following the Nazi armies' annexing Austria and Hungary, earlier having read Hemingway's *For Whom the Bell Tolls*, and the history of the Spanish war used by both Nazi and Allied nations as a warm-up for what would follow. We expected the sequel to World War I to be bloodier. We took it for granted the United States would and should rise in defense of the free world, whose standing champion was the beleaguered British. Clearly another factor was also at play: Hitler's unbridled, mounting ego, with the sidebar of rendering the Jews extinct via racial cleansing. Of the latter we knew nothing in 1940, while Hitler's desire for global conquest was common knowledge.

Many of us had serious misgivings with respect to FDR, for he took two near diabolical and conflicting stances on joining the war, declaring, "No American soldier shall cast a drop of blood on foreign soil," even while he and Winston Churchill were widely perceived to be drawing us into the conflict as fast as they could. We understood Churchill's lack of ambivalence and reasons for survival, while to me and most of my friends, FDR appeared two faced and therefore unprincipled; some felt him too conflicted to lead. At that time we were sending humanitarian and war supplies to Britain by our merchant marines that daily were being torpedoed by submarines, blasted by the Germans' surface navy and air attack.

Totally unprepared for war, isolationist, with a meager standing army, the U.S. had begun a buildup of military hardware.

The draft was passed while many young men my age began to volunteer. Some men, foreign to Yale's college ranks, were already in training in New Haven. Eventually the United States was to have 12 million men and women in uniform, backed by massive employment, largely of women in factories across the nation.

For me, it was difficult to adjust to Yale in my freshman year. Caught in conflicting emotions, thoughts, and endless dorm discussions, I found it hard to settle down to study and concentrate—and my grades reflected the impact of transition.

Rereading my diaries sixty-plus years later, three observations stand out: the depth of my high school relationships and the new friendships formed on campus; the level of activity, which was almost frenetic; and the cost—back then, $900 a year covered tuition, room, and board.

For most of my hometown friends, the college transition seemed smooth, they more readily adapted to college studies and got grades higher than mine in freshman year. Compared to me, my peers had led more rounded lives. This included more travel in the United States and abroad, more interaction with girls, and more overnights away from home. I had grown up on a farm in Minnesota. College in the east may not have represented to many the quantum leap that it did for me. They adapted more readily to factors of which I was largely unaware and therefore oblivious. I began to open up to new realities and opportunities away from home and in the east.

In my freshman year I laid a base for later years. The Yale library drew me increasingly, but I also learned jujitsu, took boxing lessons, became a squash player, played intramural baseball, and swam. I traveled to New York City, went to plays, took dancing lessons, passed my freshman courses, and learned to fly. My name even showed up on the Dean's list. But I still had lots of growing up to do. At age twenty-two I would be flying a four-engine bomber, responsible for the well-being of a crew of ten and for helping kill the Japanese who sought to kill us.

Following our freshman year, a friend, Ken Dayton, and I packed sleeping bags and gear into his green Oldsmobile sedan and drove west, through the Dakotas, then on to Yellowstone National Park, driving the narrow and awesome, winding roads of the Rockies to magnificent Glacier National Park (the first glacial ice I'd seen). It was here that I caught my first rainbow trout, which we ate at our campfire dinner. We went on to Washington, Oregon, and the magnificent Yosemite National Park.

Throughout our journey to that point, war news had been mounting. Italy had joined the war against Great Britain. Churchill scolded Benito Mussolini over the radio, as an "infamous jackal" who had "stabbed Britain in the back."

We continued on to Los Angeles and Newport Beach, where I first experienced deep-sea fishing, including extreme seasickness. I retched and fell asleep on a coil of rope. After the fog lifted, I awoke to having been burned and blistered under the sun's rays. On we drove to the shores of Lake Mead, the Grand Canyon, Bryce and Zion National Monuments. In Colorado we toured Mesa Verde and Rocky Mountain National Park, and splurged at the Broadmoor Hotel in Colorado Springs.

For the balance of the summer, I spent several weeks at Harrison and Smith, actually selling a few printing orders—shades of the days when Ken Dayton and I had sold ads for the Blake yearbook, Callopan, during our senior year. During the latter part of the summer, Charlie Cole, Dad's successor, had walked me into his office after I'd been selling small printing orders for a few weeks, suggesting he'd like me to join him after I had

Picnicking at Yellowstone National Park.

graduated from college, at Harrison and Smith. If I declined, he would make his plans to train his son-in-law, Bill Owen. I thanked him and declined his offer, noting that I thought I wanted to do something on my own.

On Sunday, December 7, 1941, in New Haven I drove into Lawlor's Garage, where the ashen-faced garage owner, John Lawlor, told me that the Japanese had bombed Pearl Harbor. A few hours later, Abe Sheldon, Phil Duff, Bud Howe, and I were on our way to the New Haven train station, New York City, and Times Square, where pandemonium reigned. We proceeded by coach to Washington, D.C., where we knew Roosevelt would call for a joint session of the Senate and House for the U.S. declaration of war. Meanwhile, students at Yale went wild, crowding before President Charles Seymour's home. He came forth to speak to them while we were Washington-bound.

After sleeping on park benches in our winter overcoats, on Monday morning we went to see our Minnesota Third District Congressman, Richard Gale, and garnered passes to the joint

Outside the Capitol when FDR declared war.

session of Congress. To be on the safe side, we also visited our U.S. Senator, Joe Ball, who issued us passes as well.

They didn't work; too many passes had been issued for the limited seats and standing room. We did join the throng lining the streets, and with my trusty Leica camera I snapped pictures of the president's limo, close enough to recognize him inside. For a reason I've never understood, an angry policeman grabbed my camera, tore out the film, and handed it back. We made our way back to Senator Ball's office, where we listened with his staff to history in the making, before returning to New Haven. The United States declared war on Japan, then on Germany and Italy. FDR had ended his ambivalence.

The pace quickened and real change set in. U.S. preparedness had begun from so far behind the goal line that the preparations required both policy and strategic planning. Meanwhile Britain and the United States had decided to go cross channel into Germany before knocking out Japan, while trying to help

Elizabeth McCabe with my friend Charlie Mead.

Russia, which Hitler had invaded. The only certainty at the time was acceleration. We had to build everything that was going to be needed in war for the British, Russians, and Americans.

Meanwhile, the rest of my bright college years gave way to other opportunities. My grades rapidly improved even as I was helping the local farmers' pear and apple picking on a piece-work basis, followed by working four hours at night and eight hours on Saturdays, making magneto coils for U.S. merchant ships at New Haven's Acme Tool & Wire Company. My wage was 60¢ per hour until I reached quota production levels and my pay increased to 75¢.

My social life changed as well. Home for Christmas holidays, I attended a Westminster Presbyterian Church luncheon put on by the minister, Dr. Lowe, for college students and those about to enter college. Across from me at the table sat blonde, blue-eyed, and beautiful Elizabeth McCabe. I later called one or two dozen McCabes in the Minneapolis phone directory before learning her address was in Bloomington. We dated a few times and any interest I had in other girls promptly vanished. It was again love at first sight on my part—later, as our relationship advanced, she acknowledged similar feelings. On September 25, 1942, near Wells College in Aurora, New York, where Elizabeth was a freshman, we became engaged. I pinned my Beta Theta Pi fraternity pin on her blue sweater. And during the abbreviated summer vacation period that enabled Yale to stay open year-round, my father married Margie Dameron, on July 4, 1942.

Primary training Fort Stockton, Texas 1943.

FLIGHT SCHOOL

HAVING DECIDED I WANTED TO serve my country as a combat pilot, I resolved to join the U.S. Army Air Corps. I did not relish landing a plane on the limited confines of aircraft carriers. This may have been a good decision: I lived through the war, and in more than 3,500 hours of flight time tossed my cookies only once, after relieving our B-24 tail gunner, Vince Sarnicola, in the turret after he had succumbed to vertigo, bouncing and firing at targets from an altitude of 300 feet.

Chuck Arnao and I enlisted at Fort Snelling in Minnesota; we were sworn in together to the Air Corp Reserves before returning respectively to Amherst and Yale, until we were called up.

During the summer of 1942, a number of our college friends visited and rotated among Ken Dayton's, Abe Sheldon's, Phil Duff's, and my home—friends and all were impressed with the charm and beauty of Elizabeth McCabe: "Izzy, the glorious one," nicknamed "Wheathead" by Brooks Fields, going with "Beethead" (me).

After I was called to active duty in March 1943, Elizabeth sent me great letters and we had occasional phone calls. But

In the cockpit of the PT-13 Primary Trainer.

when she visited me in Texas, she said she had been dating a Marine Corps pilot and captain at Minneapolis's Wold-Chamberlain Field Training Center. Months later she returned the engagement ring that had belonged to my mother; I carried a torch for her through the war. My favorite song started, "I'm going to buy a paper doll that I can call my own, a doll that other fellows cannot steal."

It was not easy to serve as Milt Williams's best man, or for that matter as Joe Sharpe's or Nick Duff's (Phil's brother) when the latter married Abe Sheldon's sister, Anne. Williams and Duff were married in the same church Elizabeth and I had selected some months earlier.

In 1943, despite a lifelong aversion to flying, my father crawled into my trainer plane, a Piper Cub, and seemed to enjoy our sightseeing trip as my first passenger after I obtained my pilot's license under the auspices of the Civilian Pilot Training Program, courtesy of Uncle Sam, with ground school linked to Yale. When we landed, although Dad was enthusiastic, noting the flight was great, he was too considerate to kiss the ground. His pride was genuine, and he understood why I'd enlisted to fly in the air corps.

Although my air corps training was all encompassing, kindly mothers near various Texas training bases gave picnics and hosted parties as part of their war effort. After graduating and attending several weeks of instructor's flight school at Randolph Field in San Antonio, I returned to instruct cadets on the verge of either being washed out or obtaining their wings. Since I had graduated only a few months earlier, the cadets found it easier to learn from me. The majority of them passed their final check ride after a few flying hours and graduated with wings.

My status was a bit of an honor, in that those who graduated in the top 10 percent from pilot training were eligible for select assignments. I wanted to fly either P-38 twin engine/twin tail fighters or medium B-25 bombers but Lubbock Base Commander Colonel Holmes, whose charming daughter Marge I'd been dating, suggested I might want to instruct for a while—which could lead to my getting my preferred aircraft assignment. I took his advice.

She had attracted my attention at a dance, as she dropped the arm of her escort as he handed her coat to one of the coat-check girls. Noting that the couple danced well but were not romantically close, I had reason for caution and encouragement. Meanwhile, a captain whom none of us knew tried to cut in on a cadet dancing with a lovely girl, who was wearing his engagement ring and dancing very close and very well. When the offensive captain took the cadet by the shoulder and noted he wanted to dance with his girl, the cadet knocked the captain cold to the floor. Not wanting that to happen to me, I didn't cut in on Marge's partner. When the dance ended, her date joined the waiting line for coats but I vaulted the counter, picked up her coat, blew the counter girl a kiss, and walked toward Marge. "I've got your coat; do I get the girl?" She laughed, and we left the dance together. Marge and I had good times together, but "no hands below the waist" was regrettably in full force.

A month later, as I was preparing to graduate from flight school, Marge pinned my wings on my new officer's uniform, and a day later, on May 23, my sister Ruth, having arrived from New York City for the occasion, repinned me, and many of us went off base for dinner.

On leave for but three days at home, except for a single date, my contacts were primarily with older adults, my counterparts having been scattered to winds and wars and across continents, while college girls were not yet out of school for the summer. I visited with the McCabes at their home, where Ben McCabe, on learning I had no intention of joining Harrison and Smith if I made it back from the war, asked that I join him in the grain business. He had been impressed by my having sent war bonds home to Elizabeth and that I didn't want to marry or have a child until I returned from combat and was earning a living. "Mother" McCabe, who wrote me often overseas, as did several other mothers, was wonderfully warm, yet a bit nostalgic as well.

I walked and talked with "Mother" Ruth Stevens, "Mother" being Brooks Fields's assigned prefix to all the mothers of the girls we knew and dated.

It was a busy three days with Dad's business associates as well. Charlie Cole, Dad's partner, made it clear that he intended to buy Dad out of Harrison and Smith. Dad was having problems with rheumatism and had lost some of his enthusiasm at age seventy-nine. It required two more years of negotiations and reciprocal acrimony before Charlie accomplished his objective and my father retired.

During that busy period, having been assigned to Randolph

Field instructor's school, and Margie and Dad's not needing two cars, I bought Margie's fine blue 1941 Ford from her for $1,000. It would better fit my life as a flight instructor.

The realities of war struck close to home. I attended a dinner hosted by Charles Arnao Sr. and his wife, Ruth, at the Nicollet Hotel, at which their young but "grown-up" daughter was present. All three of them were deeply concerned for their son and brother, and my close friend Chuck, a B-17 bomber navigator. They had been unable to find a trace of Chuck for over two years.

I learned of the death of one of my most admired friends, Bert Martin, the much respected head boy of Blake who had preceded me to Yale a year earlier. He became an army lieutenant and was killed in action when he went back to carry out a wounded soldier. In 1942 in New Haven, Bert and I had sold war stamps and bonds on campus to help finance the war effort. Bert had been a star halfback on the Yale football team—a respected leader in every way. His death, the first of a near endless procession, hit me hard.

On Sunday, May 28, Ruth and I attended Westminster Presbyterian Church, about which I wrote in my diary:

> The sermon was largely on faith and struck home. Not to find faith on an intellectual basis—we do not take medicine knowing all its properties.

My sister Ruttie and I spent hours talking about our philosophies of life. She was concerned lest I be overly fatalistic, or somehow had either a premonition or death wish, in wanting to fly combat. We are in part actuated by glory yet mindful of our objectives when blessed with values and a sense of purpose. Premonition? No. High risk? Yes. Americans had fought and died for their country. To win wars, people kill and are killed. I assumed the odds for a combat pilot to be fifty-fifty, worse were we to bomb Germany, better in the Pacific theater, though those odds on many missions looked bleak to me at best. I thought Ruttie's approach more one of emotional concern, and of love, but remote from that to which many were deeply committed to fight for their country.

Meanwhile, in the bigger world, life and lives and deaths were moving on. In Rochester, Minnesota, Dad and Margie had spent three weeks at the Mayo Clinic for Dad's severe rheumatism. He recovered, returning to Wayzata and greater pressure from Charlie Cole to sell out—an uncomfortable time for him, particularly because he had worked all his life. He continued to play handball until age eighty. Later, Charlie Cole, years younger than Dad, sold Harrison and Smith to Bemis Bag Company, one of Dad's former customers. Almost thirty years later, in the late '60s when Apache was building a conglomerate, I would gladly have acquired Harrison and Smith if I could have.

In uniform.

JOURNEY TO THE HOT WAR

AS MY TRAINING AND INSTRUCTING wore on in Texas in mid 1944, I learned that another close friend and pilot had now been killed. Tink Conner, with whom I had trained, bade me farewell in May and had gone quickly through B-24 transition school in Kansas. He was killed in an early raid on the Ploesti oil fields of Romania, the source of much Nazi oil, vital to their refineries, particularly in the German invasion of Russia.

What would have occurred had I gone to B-24 transition with Tink? Irrelevant—I didn't. In the massive air raids conducted on Europe, British bombers flew night missions, which required fewer planes, whereas the United States, by then with many more bombers and crews, took the massive daylight air raids. Chuck Arnao, a second lieutenant navigator, was shot down on his first mission, a flight of several hundred B-17s. The planes had been ordered to "go around," which they did on a forty-five-minute bomb run, slow-flying ducks for massive antiaircraft fire.

General Curtis LeMay, air force "supremo," seemed to us in the Pacific theater to put the needs of his ego ahead of his crews' survival, sentencing them to death on long, straight, and level bombing runs. After Germany's 1945 surrender, he took over the Far East air command and, as in the case of General MacArthur, found great conflict with his overdeveloped ego.

For our smaller squadrons in the Pacific theater, our bomb runs, on which we flew "straight and level," normally lasted one and a half minutes, which allowed us to take flak-evasive action while still permitting our bombardiers time to aim in their bomb sights before "bombs away." We did not have the planes or the crews to emulate the European theater's saturation bombings or sustain their massive crew and plane casualties. Our situation resulted from Churchill and Roosevelt's decision first to cripple the Nazis by air, invade and knock Germany out of the war, and only then deal with Japan, a strategy we respected and did not second guess.

As the weeks went on at Lubbock, I tired of the routine, able to understand that the developing crew shortages meant heavy bombers for me anyway. My assignment quickly followed by way of California.

Due to Dad's protracted stay at the Mayo Clinic, I had applied for emergency leave of a week's home visit, which came through the Red Cross. Among the many things I did during the leave was to sign a certificate for 163 shares of First Bank stock so that it would not have to be probated in the event of my death. After a short stint at a base in Lemoore, California, I was assigned as copilot to a crew of ten men based at March Field at Riverside, an hour and a half from Los Angeles.

In that short home leave I also learned that one of my very closest friends at Yale, Charlie Mead, had "bought the farm" in flying combat in his P-51 fighter plane. My last letter from him, written from England following his training in Florida, noted he had had two dogfights over England. He had enclosed his remaining gas ration stamps—I wept. Years later at Westminster Abbey, I found his name in the very large leather volume comprising American fliers who had died in the Battle of Britain.

I joined my crew at March Field and began flying and gunnery practice. I also began occasionally dating in L.A. one Virginia Christie, "Ginia," with whom I first enjoyed the ultimate intimacy. After all, it would have been a shame to have died in combat a virgin despite the constricted, for some of us, mores of the times. Thanksgiving of 1944 I spent with another close air corps friend, Angelo Columbo, who had flown home to San Rafael from P-47 fighter training in Louisiana. His Italian parents were wonderful, warm hosts who made and stored outstanding red wine in their basement.

Finally, two B-24 crews of us flew out of Hamilton Field in San Francisco at eleven p.m. Sunday, November 26, 1944, on our way to the hot war. We were ferried in a C-54 transport plane. By then, my closest friend on the crew was our bombardier, Roy Niemeyer, a friendship that carried over for nearly sixty years, until he suffered a fatal aneurism at our fishing lodge near Sioux Narrows, Canada, in the presence of longtime friends Neil Crain and Hans Hansen. Hans had served in the tank corps under Generals Clarke and Patton—his medals included two Purple Hearts. Commenting on a third wound he survived, I asked Hans where his third Purple Heart was. (He joked that he lacked senator and then presidential candidate John Kerry's press corps!) What joy the four of us shared over the decades!

En route to combat, a fourteen-hour flight, our two crews landed at Hickam Field, Honolulu, adjacent to Pearl Harbor, still at that time host to the lingering cadavers of battleships, cruisers, and destroyers sunk on December 7, 1941. (Decades later I flew back to Hawaii, en route to the Far East from Houston, traveling over 1,000 miles farther in Apache's Gulfstream IV, and in about seven hours' less time.)

As we were to leave Hawaii, the number 2 engine caught fire on takeoff and we braked to a stop. We spent most of our days until Sunday Dec. 3rd on Waikiki Beach. On the previous day we had listened on the radio (no TV yet) to the Army-Navy football game won by Army 23-7, and drank 25¢ Hiram Walker scotches on the beach. From Hawaii we gassed in the Johnston Islands, landed at Tarawa, where more friends had lost their lives, then at Guadalcanal, where the hulls of disabled vessels and landing barges blasted by the Japanese were much in evidence.

From there we went on to Hollandia and Biak en route to our base at Nadzab, New Guinea. At one gas stop, while standing in the chow line, I noted an emaciated, walking skeleton of a Japanese soldier in an oversized, faded uniform, hoping to be fed. An MP pulled him out of the line and used his .45 caliber revolver to blow him away. The stranger had been an enemy infiltrator. I had witnessed my first combat killing—more followed.

Christmas at Nadzab—torrential rains; hordes of mosquitoes so noisy they kept us awake at night; hot, wet clothing and cots—lacked much that we had enlisted to fight for. We were long on dysentery, short on toilet paper . . . to the point where I read avidly in the giant, roofless outhouse, tearing off paperback pages to keep pace with the "trots." Despite these negatives, Christmas Day 1944 had its redeeming features. Somehow turkeys had arrived from Australia, and loved ones and friends from home had sent packages, and hell, even the mail had caught up with us!

We did need to be careful about what we reported, for U.S. censors read our outgoing letters. Nor was our military favorably disposed to our keeping detailed diaries, lest they fall into enemy hands. Accordingly, my daily diary was understated, though I did have a code for the weight of the bombs dropped on combat missions.

Nadzab was a staging area for things to come. We did some flying, but mostly we heard from men who had seen extensive combat, some of whom had been captured, tortured, and somehow escaped. In Nadzab we unlearned much of that which we had been taught in U.S. training, particularly as concerned what to do if shot down and taken prisoner. Bombardier Roy Niemeyer and I concluded we would not be taken prisoner, nor would we commit suicide. We armed accordingly, flew without dog tags or other evidence of said number, in my case 02058084. We were invariably so hungry that once airborne and headed to the target in loose formation to save gas, we ate our C rations before climbing up and flying formation to give us coverage against the Zeros. We would then space our birds for maximum impact on the target.

Our first run against the Japanese almost proved our last, not due to enemy fire but rather, to the war-weary aircraft we flew in New Guinea. Our target, several hundred miles away, was an imposing Red Cross hospital that intelligence personnel had determined to be occupied by Japanese. We were the last of several B-24s in the mission sent to take out the target.

Unfortunately, carrying eight 1,000-pound bombs, our near wreck of a plane could not achieve maximum takeoff power, and despite revving up the engines to full throttle before releasing the brakes, we were slow to pick up speed. Beyond the end of the poor runway, an oil derrick awaited us. Lacking time and space to cut power and brake, as had the pilots on the takeoff from Hawaii, pilot Ed Ross hauled back on the steering wheel before we reached flying speed. Heart in my mouth, I thought we'd take out the derrick and crash into the low hills. Ed raised the left wing, and we cleared the oil derrick, but the plane was too slow in the climb to join the other six.

Our next emergency soon followed, as we were flying through heavy cloud cover. Off our right wing, through a break in the clouds, I noted a green wooded mountain towering above us. I poked Ed's right shoulder, and he quickly turned left and shouted to navigator George Stark, whose maps failed to reveal both where we were and the altitudes necessary to clear poorly mapped obstacles. Luckily, we were not in a box canyon, and eventually we broke out of the clouds and went on to the target. The other planes had turned back; we went in alone, dropped our bombs, but carefully spared the field hospital with its giant red cross on the roof. Whether Roy blew up anyone in the area, we did not note.

When we returned late to base, we had already been reported MIA—missing in action. That night Tokyo Rose, of melodious, soft voice and perfect English, an American record spinner and propagandist, claimed a kill, luckily in error. The guys at the base enthusiastically welcomed us to our "home away from home."

Enough "staging"—we headed to Biak, where we holed up briefly, before being transferred to our beautiful little island home, Owi. There we pitched our tents among palm trees on a magnificent white sand beach, made tables of bomb crates, swam, turned yellow from malaria-inhibiting Atabrine tablets, and nearly starved. Scouts had learned of a naval storage depot, but we had been turned away at the fenced gates, which were guarded day and night. To cope with increased hunger hardly alleviated by powdered eggs, someone came up with a great idea: to go by sea. In the plane and equipment graveyard, we "rescued" several beat-up aluminum wing tanks, which we opened up to the point that, with our hewn-wood paddles, we could glide our "canoes" across the water to the depot. The strategy worked to perfection: three little canoes at a time filled with canned food. Life was looking up!

And we flew—loose formation, tight formation "practice flights," 50 and 100 feet above the water. Natives lived from the sea; fishing was their way of life. They got about in high-masted sailboats, often in groups of up to a dozen. We did not shoot them, but flying in loose formation, we did pass low over their sails to tumble them into the water, from which they were adept at righting their craft. We were low enough, though, to note their shaking fists.

We would also fly in formation at low altitude, close enough to clip the tops off the pine trees. Regrettably, some of the clippings from our props, like grass from rotary lawn mowers, found their way into the giant engine nacelles, to the consternation of the absolutely outstanding ground crews. They didn't mind patching flak or bullet holes or frequently changing tires. But pine cuttings in the engine cells? No more shearing off treetops.

COMBAT AND THE ATOMIC BOMB

IN 1945, THE PACE OF the air war in the Pacific heated up for the Sixty-Fourth Squadron of the Forty-Third Bomb Group of the Fifth Air Force, commanded by General George Kenney. Successively we moved from Owi to Leyte, to Mindoro, and from there to Clark Field, each of those bases in the Philippine Islands. From these three bases, we flew several support missions for troops landing on Mindanao and Luzon; we bombed Corregidor on several short missions. Controlled initially by Americans, it fell to the Japanese, who drove the survivors on the Bataan Death March. Prisoners were starved and butchered en route. Some historians have termed this the greatest defeat in our history.

General MacArthur had been rescued by boat ahead of the fall of Corregidor, and was later to proclaim to history, "I shall return." He did, and led U.S. occupation forces in Japan following its surrender. In the Korean War, he took command of American and a few Allied forces, turning the tide of battle against North Korea, before President Harry Truman found it necessary to curb MacArthur's ambitions—Truman did not want to precipitate all-out war between the United States and China or Russia.

We also flew a few long night missions, such as to China's Japanese-occupied Hainan Island. But our primary targets were on Formosa, now Taiwan. By the end of 1944, U.S. air and naval power had depleted the Japanese navy and dominated the airspace in the Pacific. However, Formosa, with its airfields and strategic location in the South Pacific, remained a threat to shipping, and we were island-hopping closer to Japan, bringing up ground troops and bombers. Formosa was furiously defended by extensive antiaircraft fire power, with radar controlled capability. We were particularly fortunate that by 1945, few Japanese fighter planes were available to rise and attack us like wounded ducks from the air, which would have spelled adios, life. Nonetheless, the Japanese did rise to meet us on a few occasions. Their planes were largely used to bomb our ground positions at night. They also dropped paratroopers from air transports to attack us on the ground, and on their first night mission to our newly occupied Tacloban base at Leyte, they destroyed a number of our planes in their ground revetments.

It was while attacking Formosa airfields, from runways to antiaircraft and plane revetments, that I came to believe the odds of survival had shrunk well below 50 percent. The odds of our planes going in on the target first, with the enemy unawares, were proportionately smaller on larger bomb runs. By the time we had seen two or three squadrons approach the target under heavy antiaircraft fire, we had a good idea of the intensity of the antiaircraft fire we'd encounter at our altitude.

Meanwhile, the Japanese on the ground also had a pretty good idea of the altitude the U.S. bombers would be likely to fly, and they could and did carpet fire at us, as well as we might have carpet bombed our target. Usually their antiaircraft firing revetments were secondary targets to the planes, runways, and facilities. On shorter missions, our medium-range bombers, such as the B-25s and B-26s, could and would attack their antiaircraft revetments, sometimes aided by U.S. single-engine P-47s and twin-engine fighter bombers, the P-38s. On longer flights, such as from the Philippine bases on Luzon and Mindoro, the heavy B-24s flew 400 to 600 miles to targets that were beyond the range at which the fighter planes and light bombers could defend the heavies or disable and destroy the sources of antiaircraft fire.

It was on those longer flights that all hell broke loose, and half or more of the B-24s on the raid were struck by flak, caught fire, lost engines, and occasionally were blown apart. Of the forty missions I flew, our squadron was shot up on nineteen, and occasionally every plane in our squadron was struck by ground-based antiaircraft fire. Three of the planes I piloted, while able to make it back, were relegated to being sources of replacement parts and never flew again.

I flew on the squadron leader's right wing. We'd gotten good enough in practice formation flying that we could tap the top of the wing of the adjacent bird without scratching it; this was hair-raising at first, and thrilling, except to the frightened crew. On combat bomb runs, depending on the bombs we were dropping, we were generally about 50 feet from our next ship. I found a practical way to avoid distraction on bomb runs in heavy flak. I would sink down several inches in my seat so that shells exploding below were not going to divert my attention from maintaining our wing position. When at the controls of the plane, and when feeling the B-24 hit as we often did, most pilots would move the stick and the rudders to obtain a quick read on whether we still had effective flight control.

On one mission, a shell passed through our right-wing fuel

Posing next to a well decorated bomber.

tank without exploding (which would have destroyed us), but there were other problems: the loss of that engine, and a hole on the top of the wing so large that the rubber tank seal did not eliminate gasoline leakage and fire hazard. Realizing we would be running out of fuel on our long return to base, we immediately feathered the right outboard engine to lessen the drag of the idle propeller and the hazard of an engine spark near the gaping hole.

Three of ten crew were wounded that day, and all returned to the States. They were the only casualties our crew suffered in the war. After a difficult landing at home base, the ground crew counted 367 holes in our noble, mortally wounded B-24, which was retired to spare parts.

When the United States dropped the first atomic bomb on Hiroshima on August 6, 1945, news spread like wildfire. Official word reached us promptly both from base bosses, President Truman's confirmation, and our favorite propagandist, Tokyo Rose, constant radio spinner of great music of the era. I well recall her words on the evening of that fateful Hiroshima atom-bombing day, "Now you boys have gone and done it. But we're not through with you yet. Dig your shelters deeper, check your gas masks. We're coming for you!" said she in her sultry, mellifluous voice.

Base reaction was immediate. We were promptly issued gas masks and told to dig trenches deeper against possible gas attacks and suicide bombing runs, which had previously focused on shipping off Okinawa. We'd observed these attacks on missions from Ie Shima, my last base before returning stateside.

When Lieutenant Colonel Paul Tibbets's Enola Gay incinerated Hiroshima, killing approximately 135,000 from 30,000 feet, our flight missions had been cancelled without explanation. We were quick to comprehend why, after hearing the news. Accordingly, when on August 8 our missions were again cancelled for the next morning and we were ordered to remain out of the airspace for the second time, on penalty of being court martialed; Joe Sharp and I assumed the cancellation for a second time meant another atomic bomb.

In the interim we had engaged in an endless bull session: speculation and conjecture, absent the facts. We thought that if the United States had enough of the dread bombs, Japan would have to capitulate quickly. There were rumors that the U.S. had a list of some seven additional cities to be pulverized one at a time, to underscore the futility of continuing the slaughter.

We were grateful that Truman had the courage to order the attack, believing he was well advised that the death losses on both sides would be reduced were Japan's invasion removed from the agenda of moving men and materials to nearby bases for the final, costly assault which could have made the bloody battles for Luzon, Tarawa, Guadalcanal, Tinian, Iwo Jima, and Okinawa resemble picnics, except for those involved. Death estimates had run from 1 to 5 million military and civilians. And the odds, if Japan could be intimidated into surrender, made our prospects for returning stateside alive much brighter.

At the same time, our guys were somber. The world, we clearly comprehended, was somehow going to have to learn to live with the new issue of the threat of extinction of human life and civilization as we knew it. Following the Enola Gay's first strike, I had penned the cheerful note that the atomic process might well lead to more efficient energy for use in power and locomotion.

I wrote in my diary:

August 8, 1945

> I did little today except copy the writing I did last night. It still sounded like a good thought today—point lying in attempted logic that now more than ever before, adherence to the principles and teachings of Christ opposing to those of indifference are necessary to combat a world where an atomic bomb has been possible.

On August 9, Joe Sharpe, with whom I'd trained in Texas, and served as best man at his wedding, flew over from Okinawa to pick me up in his C-46 transport plane, air space over Japan having closed for the atomic bomb. As we came in for landing on Okinawa, a Japanese Zero buzzed us—then turned away. We took a jeep, drove through the utter devastation, noting only one church steeple standing in a several block area, and went to his mess hall for lunch at Naha, Okinawa.

On what was to be our short flight back to Ie Shima, seated

next to each other as Joe flew his plane, we discussed straying to the north to see if we could find any evidence of the second atomic bomb. Not wanting the evidence of "straying from course" in my diary, I omitted the account from the day's entry, but not the memory.

We had flown possibly 200-plus miles and were becoming a bit nervous, when there ahead of us was the giant mushroom cloud, rising from the remnants of the beautiful city of Nagasaki. I had previously flown two missions over it; on both flights we took heavy antiaircraft fire. I remembered how impressed I had been when surveying the city from the air, seeing the lush green mountains contrasting with the deep blue water and white cumulus clouds. We turned toward Ie Shima and flew back to base in awed silence.

Later reports estimated that of the pre-bomb population of Hiroshima of 255,000 casualties claimed 135,000 lives, including deaths later due to radiation; the smaller population of Nagasaki, more protected by mountainous terrain, lost approximately 64,000 citizens—and lost the war for the Empire of Japan.

The Nagasaki flight crew of The Great Artiste B-29 bomber was Major Charles W. Sweeney, age twenty-five. Both its and the Enola Gay's mission had involved multiple B-29s, weather ships, damage assessment people, observers, and technicians. An observer in the plane following The Great Artiste described the base of the rising column to be about 3 miles long, tapering off at the top to about a mile, the bottom brown, the center amber, and the top white. "Then, just when it appeared as though the thing had settled down, there came shooting out of the top a giant mushroom that increased the pillar to a total of 45,000 feet—more alive than the pillar, seething and boiling in a white fury of creamy foam, sizzling upward and then descend-

Japanese bombers (with black crosses) arriving preliminary to the surrender.

ing earthward, a thousand Old Faithful geysers rolled into one."

Sure enough, the Japanese prepared to capitulate following Nagasaki. On Monday, August 20, a number of us went to the flight line where we had observed two or three Japanese "Betty" bombers, painted white with black crosses, landing at Ie Shima en route to a surrender-planning session on a base to the south. I snapped pictures of the planes coming in to land. They parked near enough that I also recorded the shorter Japanese diplomats being received by American rank, among whom must have been the tallest men available for the preliminary historic occasion. Sixty years later I retrieved some of those photos.

Two days previously I had received a letter from my step-mother, Margie that had touched me and may have been a por-tent of my first marriage to Sally Stevens. I had written in my diary on August 18, 1945:

Margie wrote of Sal's having walked home with Dad. Visualizing her walking with Dad either through the little white gate or along the driveway strikes tenderly close—so many times I've watched Dad's hand wave, the broad smile beneath his summer straw hat, and the, "Hello everybody, hello Ray." It's touching to think of Sal being there too, on his birthday.

Although the war was over, death still stalked, following President Truman's announcement on August 15 that Japan had accepted American peace terms. An entry from my diary reads:

We had an alert tonight, learned a Jap plane had dropped bombs—vast celebration at home (States). Dark tonight (no lights to guide bombers).

On August 28 I lost yet another good pilot friend, Captain Sill. Flying a B-32 to Japan with twenty-two personnel for a planned broadcast over Tokyo, he lost two engines and crashed; a tragic death of a grand personality and a loyal, devoted husband. By September 10, my stateside orders had come through, and having finished up most of the citations (I was the group's citations officer), I went to see if Major Parker would release me to hitchhike to Manila for the long boat ride to San Francisco and then to Fort MacArthur, near Los Angeles.

To return stateside for rotation leave, we needed to earn 100 points. Doing so read like a death wish: one point for each five hours of combat flight, one point for each mission on which a squadron plane was struck by enemy antiaircraft fire, five points for surviving a bailout by parachute or crash landing on shark infested ocean or a crash landing other than on "home base." I averaged 2 ½ points per mission and 100 points by 43rd Bomber Group count. But I received only 97 points by discharge base count.

We had drawn enemy fire that apparently had not been counted at the California Fort MacArthur discharge base. On that tense day, a major bargained hard, offering me my captaincy were I to reenlist in the National Guard or U.S. Army Air Force Reserve pool. My argument was brief and to the point. If I deserved the promotion from first lieutenant to captain, then grant it. If not, I did not cotton to two weeks per year of annual training that would interrupt my civilian life and leave me dangling like a puppet on a string. I thought my duty to my country had been fulfilled; I had miraculously survived, thank God, and had lots of catching up to do with those who had desk jobs and a four-year civilian jump-start. Furthermore, and unspoken, I had a date with Ginia in Los Angeles before catching a train home. That was my business, not the major's. He granted me an honorable discharge on the spot.

I did not stop to pick up the majority of my campaign ribbons for the numerous theaters in which I had served. I recoiled at wearing several rows of them, and anyway, I had enough to mount in Lucite for future reference. What would I do with them? Use them as date bait? Wear them on the Yale campus as I completed my senior year?

Sixty five years later, in reading English author Max Hastings's *Retribution: The Battle for Japan 1944–1945*, I noted where an American B-29 had made it back to base with some six hundred holes from bombing Japan. It's quite a read. So is Laura Hillenbrand's *Unbroken: A World War II Story of Survival, Resilience, and Redemption*. *Why Courage Matters*, by Senator John McCain, who as a prisoner of war did not break down under physical abuse in the Vietnam War, also resonates with my own perspective:

We are taught to understand, correctly, that courage is not the absence of fear, but the capacity for action despite our fears. We need it because without courage, all virtue is fragile, admired, sought, professed, but held cheaply and surrendered without a fight. Courage is what Winston Churchill called "the first of human qualities . . . because it guarantees all the others." We can admire virtue and abhor corruption sincerely, but without courage we are often corruptible. Daniel Webster said, "A sense of duty pursues us ever." So it is with the debts we owe to the brave, the obligation to repay courage with courage.

We boarded a cramped troop ship with two bent screws driving the ship, which plowed sideways across the water from October 6 through 28, until we passed under the Golden Gate Bridge. We slept in bunks reeking of vomit—succeeding only one night to stretch out full length on deck. The rest of the trip, until we reached cooler climate, we felt abused and angry. The accompanying thought was that when needed overseas, we traveled by plane. After the war was won, we traveled by sea in a clunker unfit for cattle. Fortunately, about the time we crossed the International Date Line, the joy of surviving and reaching home overcame our self-pity and irritation, and optimism and anticipation took over.

Under Sunday, October, 28, 1945, my diary reads:

Up long before the sun, we had an enfeebled breakfast, went on deck. It was still early when the stateside friendliness began with a small ship which cruised around us with people waving, a band playing. More people waited at the dock. When we unloaded, the process was orderly, efficient, and we moved quickly to a ferry. While we lined up, Red Cross girls brought delicious cookies and coffee around. The girls smiled and some yelled, "Hey Red, I need a haircut. Will you cut my hair?"

When I made a rapid trip to quarters after landing, I was able to call Dad and Margie, who sounded wonderful. The hamburger dinner, French fries, green peas, and chocolate malt surpassed my fondest anticipation.

When Japan had attacked Pearl Harbor on December 7, 1941, I'd hastened to our nation's capital for the joint session of Congress calling for war against the Axis powers. Four years later, in August 1945, I watched the atomic bomb decimate Nagasaki, concluding one of history's bloodiest periods. And now, on Wednesday, October 31, we reached Union Station and went by two buses to Fort MacArthur at San Pedro. I was going home

Between the bookends of World War II—the Declaration of War in Washington D.C. and the decimation of Nagasaki by the second atomic bomb and subsequent Japanese surrender—the foundation came together and I was, for the first time, in charge of my personal destiny. I built the foundation for the life I've led and the personal values that drove all that followed; I was for the first time in charge of my personal destiny.

STATESIDE

WHEN I LANDED FROM THE Pacific and left the Air Force, I faced a series of alternatives about what to do next. Some of these I had previously thought through, making it easier to reject the ministrations of the military. For example, one of my earliest business partners joined the National Guard. I did not want the contingencies of recall to active duty to either interrupt or compete with the pursuit of a business career of my own design, so this path was not an option for me. I already knew I was leaving the military even before meeting my father at the Minnesota train station—the same station where we had choked back tears three years earlier.

There was also an immense flurry of contacts with girls. Some of them I had dated briefly during premilitary duty, others I had known in high school and college, and a larger, continuing set I met during the first year upon returning stateside. Whether the Harvards or Yalies drank more at the round of dorm parties, I don't recall; it was irrelevant, as were other options on my return from duty.

In Minnesota, I spent long days hunting rabbits and pheas-

Chuck Arnao and Bob Niels return from war.

ants with Bob Niels and Chuck Arnao, selling the rabbits to rural feed stores and to mink ranchers. We partied nights. It was reminiscent of our days prior to leaving for the air corps, dispersed to different geographic locations—Texas, California, and Florida. But our days were not all hunting. Twice I went to classes at the University of Minnesota with Bob Niels, who was in his senior year. Chuck Arnao had returned from having been a prisoner of war in a Nazi Stalag Luft.

Dad's associate, Charlie Cole, made one final effort to persuade me to join him at Harrison and Smith; and Ben McCabe, to join his grain business. However, I sought a career in which I would be part of starting a business, and was particularly confident that one of the larger national or international company environments was not my cup of tea.

Several of us, including Minnesotans Abe Sheldon, Phil Duff,

Roy Neimeyer after a pheasant hunt.

and Bud Howe, and Dick ("Arse") Holbrook from Michigan, spent endless days and hours exploring how to start a publication for returnees and young Americans, based in Minnesota. In the clarity of hindsight, we were intrigued with putting our energies into something we might undertake together, and a publication carried top billing. Dad had many friends, including the able secretary of state, Mike Holm, and we could also count on the parents of a number of girls we had dated, as well as our more respected peers. We discussed with them ideas for entrepreneurial careers.

There were essentially two bodies of serious thought. Many adults from their fifties into their seventies had seen the civilian economy depressed since 1930, and their outlook during a protracted world-weakened economy was that upon the return of 100 million workers to largely civilian production, the United States would fail to absorb its own 12 million in uniform. Factories full of war production would fall back into a depression,

Brooks Fields and "Arse" Holbrook at Yale.

along with the world at large.

I believed the contrary, and while agreeing that the prewar years and the presidency of Franklin Roosevelt—which, most importantly, provided hope while advancing socialism and the survival safety nets—had left more to be desired than emulated or repeated. In war we'd been exposed to so many technological advances that I believed immense application and job creation would be driven from the expanding roots of technological innovations and deferred availability of goods and services. I argued that both the Depression and the war had contributed to vast market potential, both conventional and new.

On the lengthy train ride from Los Angeles to Minneapolis, I stopped over in Omaha to visit with my very dear air corps friends, Tal and Jere Quick, who had gone into the home insulation business. For several hours we discussed their reasons for entering the business of blowing insulation from large trucks into new housing, to accommodate the already rapidly rising

My Yale graduation, 1946.

family formation demographics and demand for family housing, the construction of which was taking off. We agreed that the human energy and innovation long pent up would sweep away vestiges of the Depression. The youthful work force reservoir had given rise to many more women working, which also boded well for a dynamic economy. The two veteran generations were optimistic, energetic, and driven. For me, having survived combat in the Pacific, I felt the rest should do me well, with the wind at our backs rather than bullets in our faces.

Returning to Yale, I had the combined financial benefits of accumulated untaken leave compensation, a few weeks of unemployment compensation, and education payments under the G.I. Bill of Rights, which better prepared millions of the more serious-minded youth to urgency and an awakening sense of potential. Campus contacts with our professors, eating our meals with them during the week, playing bridge with them, and relating with them at greater depth than we had before the war were increased opportunities in peacetime.

To my immense surprise, although I spent less time on my studies in 1946 than I had previously, my absorption had grown by leaps and bounds—as did my grades. I would graduate on the Dean's List in my final post-war Yale term. My diary makes quick shrift of Yale graduation day, which my sister Ruttie attended and graced, following which we repaired to New York City.

PLANK AND SOMEKAWA

MY CLOSE FRIEND BROOKS FIELDS'S military career had followed a winding track. Nicknamed "Brooker," he found himself in the cavalry in Kansas, more constructively relevant in the wars from the era of Genghis Khan to Abe Lincoln. Although he liked horses, which did play a lingering role as the Germans sought to move equipment in the long winter campaign against Russia, he found himself studying Chinese at Cornell University. With his Yale contacts and superbly engaging personality, Yale gave him credit toward graduation, delivering his Yale degree at the Cornell campus in Ithaca, New York.

He was then assigned to the European theater, having expected to be sent to Asia. He had bumped into General Joe "Vinegar" Stillwell in California, who quickly got his orders changed to the Far East, where he spent the rest of the war caught up in the nature of the Chiang Kai-shek and Allied politically conflicted interests. Brooks returned straight to Yale from China and a tour of duty that had encompassed meetings with the author-diplomat Theodore White as well as Madame and Chiang Kai-shek.

Brooks and my desire to start a business together burgeoned. Brooks researched the Yale Placement Bureau for leads, most of which centered on large companies' recruitment and training courses, which lacked appeal. Eventually, in Hartford, Connecticut, he found the Simplex Corporation, a small business bookkeeping and accounting service, whose philosophy appealed to us both.

Simplex Corporation's president Bob Metzger held that there would be an explosion of small business formation and of family business expansions, extending to sons and relatives returned from war. The young couples, able to run the operations of restaurants, drugstores, small retail shops, service stations, garages and flower shops, offered an immense and waiting market. Why? Because the amount of record keeping, accumulation of data for tax returns, and profit and loss statements would be burdensome and boring. So would the mandated paperwork requirements of city, county, state and federal governments, bankers and insurance providers. We would offer them a simple, "handy dandy," set of daily and monthly forms to simplify their lives and meet their requirements inexpensively.

Brooks and I started researching Simplex and its principals, Victor Tantalo and his senior associate, Bob Metzger. Mr. Wilgoos, a Pratt & Whitney senior executive located in Hartford, was the father of Alice "Widgeon" Wilgoos whom I much cared for, and he ran the trap on Metzger and Tantalo, reporting positive findings. Our diligence may have been pretty good for the time and our then inexperience. Further, once we had committed and made our initial payment for the materials we would be selling door-to-door, Vic Tantalo, his wife, and five-year-old daughter drove to Minneapolis and proved most helpful as we got our business under way. In the oversimplified but useful dichotomy of "good guy, bad guy," Vic was a very good guy.

At the beach with Alice "Widgeon" Wilgoos.

August through November 1946 had provided a career starting gate.

Among the impediments we faced was inadequate transportation; neither of us had a car, and aside from socializing, we needed mobility for door-to-door selling. Brooks and I lined up access to an army surplus jeep on the Newark, New Jersey, docks. The rules we encountered didn't present much surprise; after all, we were dealing with the government, where mice had teeth and authority to exercise "where is, as is." You may open the hood; you may not start the engine. You will pay $495 in cash or certified check—neither of which we could produce.

As fate would have it, during May and June 1946, Hartford had opened new social horizons. I had been dating several young women, one being Sally Stevens. One weekend I had traveled by train to the University of North Carolina campus, where Sally was in the process of obtaining a joint master's degree in psychology and sociology. We had an outstanding time before she dropped me from her Model A Ford, leaving me to hitchhike to New York, conveyed by a speed demon even more reckless than I.

Sally had a cousin who lived in Plainfield, New Jersey, who agreed to bring $500 in cash, which I agreed to repay. When he arrived on the dock to purchase the jeep, we flashed the cash but held back until the motor started. Our ultimate topless Bluebonnet fired up in a cloud of fumes and smoke before the exhaust assumed reasonable proportions and our journey and selling plans could go forward. Safely back in Ruttie's apartment, the jeep parked for the night, we laid out our route home to our business career in Minnesota.

There was considerably more to starting our business, which we called Northwest Business Service, than calling on prospects and finding inexpensive office space. Brooks and I had talked through a plan with enough step-by-step priorities coupled with flexibility to overcome the pitfall of wondering, "What am I going to do next?" We knew what we needed to do, and had broken it down to what we would pursue individually, undertake jointly, or defer until the next steps became more obvious.

I was responsible for the legalities of incorporating Northwest Business Service with the assistance of Dad's and Harrison and Smith's legal counsel, Fred Thurber. We'd begin each owning half but would leave open a full third until Bud Howe decided whether to join us. We needed an initial board of directors. Brooks and I extended the invitation to our respective fathers, with whom we'd canvassed our plans both individually and together, during which process they became better acquainted. Both appreciated our approach; both demurred firmly.

Brooks had met, liked, and respected Dad's associate and

good friend Ed White, who happily accepted. An acquaintance of Ed was to become our first customer; Cedric Adams, the communications impresario of Minnesota (and beyond) on radio and local TV news, helped as well. Cedric wrote a widely followed news column for the area's dominant Cowles newspaper empire. Brooks and I both met with Cedric, and Brooks did an outstanding job carrying the lead in the interview. The newspaper coverage plus occasional follow-ups brought us recognition, numerous leads and customers across the state, and interviews with potential commission salespeople, whom Brooks and I interviewed separately and took to the field for trial runs.

We shared banking, and experience quickly mounted. We started with a young banking officer named Chy Hallenberg, of the First National Bank of Minneapolis. The bank had advertised its outreach to returning veterans. When Brooks saw the direction of our sales meeting with Chy, he answered the question, "What collateral do you have available to pledge?" with "Collateral, what's that? You're supposed to be lending us money in confidence that we'll pay you back as we sell these handy-dandy systems." Wrong response. Nor would Chy gamble that our beautiful red monthly ledgers or brown day books might have value to anyone other than ourselves, and definitely not the bank, the epitome of bookkeepers or bean counters. In the end, I was able to otherwise borrow money, loan half to Brooks, and we incorporated.

Later, after having developed a number of customers—who paid $10 down and $2 monthly with fees for service—we were able to assign accounts to secure working capital and reorder systems from Simplex.

Brooks's brother, Fred, had a tiny 12 by 8 foot office on the third floor of the walk-up Times Building (at 8th and Hennepin in Minneapolis) outfitted with a desk and a chair, with room for a second, folding bridge chair. For these facilities, including use of a telephone and local calls, we paid $10 per month. Our two-person staff, the elderly Mr. Lehman and Abe Sheldon's wife-to-be, Clytie (Sally's cousin), squeezed in with a card table and an adding machine (a secondhand Clary bought for $50). Clytie's and my college portable typewriters completed the initial equipment. Brooks and I agreed that we could not afford to pay ourselves above $20 per week. Until we required more space, sales meetings were held in local coffee shops and restaurants, whose Greek owners became our splendid customers. Brooks had a marvelous rapport with the proprietors.

We prospected around the clock. When we had dates, we sometimes had the girls record customer invoices. This earned them free lunches, or they helped with potential prospect mailings as we battled to progress beyond door-to-door cold calls. Sally helped, even picking apples from Dad's orchard, the receipts from which become "miscellaneous revenues." Early on, in addressing how we recorded our own profit and loss statements, I concluded that a two-year service contract for $48 was not current income; rather, we needed to amortize the deferred balance into the revenue/income stream as the monthly contracts progressed and were fulfilled. (Many years later, the outcome for Enron would have been different had it done so.)

While the approach was not encouraging during the early months, it had practical advantages: it enabled us to recognize that customers and Northwest Business interests could better be served if we broadened the services provided and folded the $2 per month contracts into the new arrangements. As the conversion of rudimentary bookkeeping to an enhanced assistance progressed, customers came to know us and were usually pleased to pay for greater value received.

We began to attract a higher order of job applicants who

liked the concepts we represented, and our early customers began to generate leads. We were getting under way, but we were still struggling with reliable transportation and even such mundane challenges as parking. Our jeep was but a fair weather, if not a hot day, friend. Mr. Lehman was none too sanguine about visiting a client, or making calls, while having to hold his fedora on his head or shiver as he drove. His allegiance deserted us by late 1946. We attempted to secure free or cheap parking by seeking to persuade the local bus people that our little blue jeep really wouldn't diminish their ability to serve the public. We wanted to house our vehicle in their terminal a block from our office; unfortunately Greyhound declined. Our jeep became more than an oddity when perched in alleys, despite the sympathies of police whose graces Brooks was adroit at enlisting. Nor could we survive our first winter. Even topless girls perform to their audiences in heated space!

We had matters to review with Simplex in Hartford, and there were personal considerations as well; Brooks, had become enamored of Martha Esser, soon to be Fields. Bud had reached Hartford ahead of us, and soon after removed himself from partner consideration. Brooks and I cemented the Hartford arrangements, signed the contract for more materials, paying over another $1,000 to Simplex, then headed for my sister Ruth's New York City apartment.

As the summer of 1946 wore on, a number of the younger businessmen, mostly veterans, formed a highly fruitful business relationship that we called the One Two Club, named for the hours of our monthly meetings, enough after most businessmen's noon hour to allow the members to keep a noon appointment and still make One Two Club meetings. The rules were that the club had to limit one member from each type of business: bank, accounting firm, employment agency, securities broker, building contractor, general insurance agency, life insurance and mortgage company, manufacturing, and an office equipment business. Each was pledged to and delivered business prospects. In addition to business luncheons, two formal events per year provided dinner and entertainment. Our new group of social contacts and friendships flourished. The group also started an investment club to which the members could invest from $10 to $100 per month. We hit several newly public companies on the rise, and the appreciation was remarkable.

During 1947, the advent of broadening accounting services and the then March 15 filing date for federal tax returns had several ramifications. I decided to go to night school to study accounting and taxes at the Minnesota School of Business. Our required reinvestment and Brooks's marriage to Martha, coupled with his remarkable selling ability, rendered Northwest Business Service too boring and the salary there too thin for him. He opted for a much higher-paying job with Pillsbury Mills, from which he then moved to Burdick Grain Company, where he quickly moved up to number two to "Big Al" Burdick, and to considerable capital growth. His success and outreach were spectacular.

Brooks and Martha remained lifelong friends, our families traveled abroad together to London, the Lowland Countries, East and West Germany, France, Yugoslavia, Hungary, Greece, and Italy. Among Brooks's and my "golden" employees—golden because they were so effective—were Clytie (Stevens) Sheldon; Lynn Lindsay, who eventually returned to his family's water-softening business; and Carl Somekawa.

Carl's family was Japanese American, U.S. citizens who had been living in California. Following Pearl Harbor, American

Carl and Mari Somekawa's wedding photo.

fears of a Japanese West Coast invasion led to confiscation of their assets and internment in the equivalent of prison camps. When freed, Carl went through the University of Minnesota, majoring and graduating in accounting. He was studying for his CPA when he interviewed for a job with us. He had been unable to obtain Minneapolis employment for which his qualifications were excellent—discrimination, a carryover from the war, prevailed.

I hired Carl promptly; he married a lovely girl named Mari and soon became my partner in Plank and Somekawa, successor to Northwest Business Service. It worked well; Carl got his CPA quickly, was warmly received among my business associates and friends (who could not have remained my friends otherwise), and I'm pleased to be able to note, handled Sally's mother's tax work until her death at age ninety-eight.

The business grew until some sixteen individual employees and hundreds of small business and tax accounts were involved. While Carl's efforts focused solely on accounting and tax, mine progressed horizontally, as I developed both a new format and strategy.

From within the One Two Club memberships, I built relationships that worked well personally and career-wise. These I formalized through the creation of several separate businesses that interlocked in the recognition of monetary rewards. First, with the help of Chuck Arnao's background in small-business finance, we formed Arnao Plank Inc., headed by Chuck, its equity owned by Chuck and me.

Next, to sell both life and general insurance, we formed Plank Anderson & Peet, bringing Chuck onto the masthead when, through Truman Anderson's Union Life Insurance Company relationship, we obtained a franchise to place and service home mortgages. It performed quite well, considering the limited time we devoted to it.

As a result of Leonard Dayton's Smith Barney employment and his brother Ward's Chicago affiliation, Leonard began to peddle interests in the drilling of oil wells. My initial interest in that business was driven by wanting to leverage Plank and Somekawa by handling the accounting and oil-related tax work of Leonard's investors. The One Two Club had taken an interest, as did I in an Illinois venture. I helped Leonard with referrals and handling the accounting work for the limited partners.

At the same time, Oklahoma promoters had invaded the metropolitan Minneapolis and suburban areas under the auspices of a General Mills officer who had married the daughter of one Bryan Pace. Pace's outreach was quickly leveraged by the respected Minneapolis attorney, Robert Flanagan, who had carefully constructed his practice by cozying up to the heirs of the Minneapolis rich and famous. I went to Bob, whom I'd met a number of times in the interest of handling the accounting for that set of investors which didn't overlap those of Leonard Dayton. Plank and Somekawa took over the setting-up of the records and their maintenance, including checking the propriety of charges levied. The two sets of relationships would lead directly to the formation of Apache.

SETTLING IN

IN THE FALL OF 1946, the busy work schedule had become busier, and by way of making room for the business, the frenetic social schedule of my evenings and weekends slowed down extensively. On December 20, Dad and I met my sister Beck, and her husband Bill Pettijohn. They brought their two children, Julia, age ten, and Tommy, age five, after spending years in South Africa. With Ruth coming from New York City on the twenty-second, it was the first time the family was together for Christmas after my mother's death in 1937—and it was great. They came by the office, shopped together, and set up the Christmas tree which Sal and her brothers, Steve and Charlie, brought in from the cold and snow. My diary noted: "Together my family, the Pettijohns and I, with Sal helping, decorated the tree, that Tommy and Julia got a great charge out of the bulbs and balls." (South Africa's Christmas drastically differs.)

Ruttie and I joined Sal and her mother for Christmas Eve church services at the Wayzata Community Church. We Planks had our Christmas in the morning, and Ruttie, whose short stay made our Christmas complete, caught the plane back to New York and work.

Over the 1946 holidays my sister Becky, Sally and her parents, and I were together frequently. We took Tommy and Julia snow sledding. The kids, intrigued with the novelty of snow, loved it—and Sally was marvelous with them. The season and the interaction impacted me greatly, and I was close to feeling and believing that Sally was the woman I wanted to marry. It took eleven months, however, for the matter to come to a head. In the interim, the little businesses grew, but not without maximum effort on my part, to the extent that even had Sally not been my chosen partner, there would have been no time for dating anyone else.

As the businesses were growing, Abe and Clytie were married in Plainfield, New Jersey, in an elaborate affair for which all the Minneapolis Yale contingent rallied: Stu Hanson, Ken Dayton, Con Brooks, Brooks Fields, David Cooper from Blake, many of Abe's college friends, Clytie's friends, including Sally, and a host of family, including numerous cousins. That took a week out of the year and was well worth it.

Brooks and Martha Esser were married in New Ulm, Minnesota; Sally and I drove down for the wedding in a snowstorm. Martha was Catholic and Brooks Christian Scientist; they were able to marry in the church chapel. I, as a Presbyterian and Brooks's best man, had to stand outside at a distinct and angry disadvantage, barred from Martha's Catholic church. That, however, was only the beginning. Two of Martha's brothers kidnapped the bride, and of course it fell on me to find and retrieve her. By the time that ignominy was repaired and Martha and Brooks were rejoined, it was very late. The newlywed Fields left in a clatter of tin cans and the shrill, frigid blast of a blizzard. They did not reach their destination, but had to spend their first night in a farmhouse along the way. Sal and I somehow made it back to our respective homes, with snowflakes blowing furiously around us.

Sally Stevens.

Abe Sheldon had left his job at the International Milling Company and started a mutual fund he named the Minnesota Fund. Having been asked to serve on his board, I did so. That business exposure proved invaluable to my then scant knowledge of how the financial world of stocks and bonds worked—"absorption learning." Later, Abe and his management company (in which I had no role) fell afoul of the Securities and Exchange Commission. He was required to give up his position in the securities business, and the other independent directors and I had the task of replacing the management company, known as Minneapolis Associates. My term as a director of the original Minnesota Fund evolved and lasted thirty-five years and through their fund management contracts, the last with Minnesota's largest insurer, the St. Paul Companies, headed by the able Carl Drake. The fund business turned out to be a tragedy for

Abe but an outstanding experience for me. It launched multiple enduring relationships along the way and built a base for later useful Apache Corporation sophistication.

Of comparable value was my experience of joining the Young Presidents' Organization (YPO), the Minnesota chapter of which had perhaps eighty members, approximately 70 percent of whom had inherited their businesses. At the time I joined the group, it was my perception that it was imbalanced toward social self-indulgence, with somewhat limited focus on how better to run and grow our businesses, participate more actively in political and community affairs, and reach out with greater innovation to minorities and the poor. With the help of the more energetic members, we were to correct this imbalance within our chapter.

Because I took a more activist role, and because of the reach of our businesses into the wide-open arenas of tax accounting (both policy and application), I was to become sought after as a director of the kinds of businesses to which I hoped to add balance and from which I might continue to expand my own broadening but still limited horizons. I accepted board positions on a St. Paul life insurance company (on which I was to serve for twenty-five years), a manufacturing company, a national wholesaler of jams and jellies ("Home Brand on the Label Means Good Food on the Table"), a high-tech computer-related company, and an international sporting goods manufacturer.

I also added an all-natural-resources mutual fund to our business repertoire. It was offered by our oil program development salesmen prior to the formation of Apache in 1954. Later I merged it into a larger Omaha fund under the auspices of the insurance company, Mutual of Omaha.

Banks were a different matter. The major Twin Cities banks, then the First National Bank and Northwestern National Bank, were the premier banks of the Ninth Federal Reserve District. Their boards were large, old line, and run by heirs of first families interlocked with the largest regional investment firms, Piper Jaffray and Dain Kalman. Their boards comprised numerous senior executives from the area's largest businesses. I was targeted as a director of a branch bank of each, but that had no appeal. I didn't want future conflicts of interest and was too small a fish for the larger banks, though appearing below their level as "a comer." "Lend yourself to all, give yourself to none" has been an abiding dictate.

I had been invited to go on the boards of the third- and fourth-largest banks in the area, and found the offers both interesting and challenging, but after due consideration I declined. This was fortunate, for the head of one group became the first interested in taking control of Apache. My position in serving on bank boards mirrors my principle at Apache. Although they may be individually experienced and qualified, I would not invite bankers, investment bankers, or practicing lawyers to serve on Apache's board, as their business or professional careers might conflict with shareholder and employees' interests.

MY FAMILY WAY

MEANWHILE, AS 1947 WORE ON, having made up my mind that Sally and I should marry, I began to become frustrated that perhaps I had missed my window of opportunity. Discussing the matter with Brooks and Abe Sheldon, Abe recommended a course that began to appeal to me.

Sal had obtained a part-time job, several days a week at the Oval Room of Dayton's, selling high-end women's attire, and while we dated, her social calendar was open—to my concern and jealousy. One thing no one expected me to give up, ever, was my love of the outdoors—hunting and fishing with numerous friends similarly inclined. Certainly, my social life needed to array itself to circumscribed forays particularly in the fall, with its majestic colors, and excursions to the Dakotas and Canada. It seemed to me I was spending more time in the field with Sal's youngest brother, Murray, than with his sister.

On a date with Sally one evening before an early-morning departure for a Dakota hunting trip, I restated my desire to marry her. Noting my return date, I suggested she might do both of us the favor of coming up with an answer while I was out of

With Sally on our wedding day.

town. Our next date was agreed upon: the night of my return, Monday, November 17, 1947. And on this date she assented.

Sally's and my engagement and wedding planning fell largely to her mother, who changed our preferred March 1948 date to June 12.

The period of our engagement saw rapid business evolution, night school, and intense tax work between mid-December and March 15.

Brooks sold his interest back to Northwest Business Service, including Carl Hanson and Stan Hagen of Plank and Some-kawa and me, for $1,695, the price we negotiated in less than an hour's discussion, following which Carl and Stan were pleased to become partners and share in the future of the growing firm.

Dad had made available to Abe and Clytie several acres adjacent to the Wayzata Community Church, where Sally and I and Abe and Clytie were to become neighbors and house our first children. Each of us selected the architect, Perry Larawa, recommended to us by the real estate division of the First National Bank's One Two Club representative, Bill Rafferty. We were delighted to wind up with two fine homes in line with our then limited purses. I financed our 26- by 36-foot Cape Cod home with a 4 percent loan, on which my payments were to be $37 monthly. It was the first house of perhaps a dozen I've caused to be built over the decades, and the only one financed with a mortgage; all other were built with personal, uncollateralized loans that I could retire on my schedule. Or I paid cash.

To establish personal credit and concurrently select two brokers I could trust, I opened small checking and savings accounts at each of several banks. I used them largely for paying for shares of stock in companies I thought would appreciate over a relatively near term. I also listened to the stock purchase proposals of a number of motivated salesmen, three of whom, with different firms, proved to be astute as well as trustworthy. When I felt my debt had risen to a caution point, I sold enough shares to liquidate all debt, pay the related taxes on net gains, and add to my "war chest" of working capital, toward which I was particularly fastidious, to the plaudits of the lenders. I became confident at handling our business and personal finances.

The combination worked well and further contributed to the growth of our business, one of which became Homes, Inc. Dad had sold a parcel of land to Chuck Arnao and me from the west side of his holdings, for $300 per acre. Chuck and I went before the Wayzata city council, registered it as a modest devel-

Newlyweds and neighbors: Abe and Clytie Sheldon with me and Sally.

opment, and arranged for city water and sewage disposal, which we contracted personally to meet local specifications. Together we brought a builder, Elton Patchell, and Sam Bowman, a lumber dealer, into Homes, Inc. Chuck and I both sold lots, while Chuck took charge of the overall development. Chuck and two accounting firm partners, Carl Somekawa and Stan Hagen, as well as Sally's brother, Charlie, a salesman for our business named Athern, and Roger LaCroix (of Paine Webber's founding lineage) became early customers, while parties unknown snapped up the remaining lots on which we built homes.

We wound up making and dividing a few thousand dollars, but not without two significant problems. First, a construction craft union picketed our development and threatened to shut down construction when we spray painted rather than hire union painters to apply paint with brushes. After earlier problems with two houses, which delayed sales and cost us money, we used no more union labor or contractors. And we lost several thousand dollars on Charlie Stevens's house; his flourishes exceeded the estimated adjusted costs that we were able to negotiate. Both Chuck and I felt that he had taken advantage of a personal and family relationship—which was his style.

These experiences afforded a chapter of lifetime learning. We had to delay payments to our contractor and materials provider, while straining credit for a period of Homes, Inc. We collapsed the company when the reasonably attractive development was completed. The owners took over their gardening and landscaping, as we had made a small parcel of land with excellent soil available to collective vegetable gardening. A number of the homeowners gardened there with appreciation.

Chuck and I had learned our lesson. On the next, considerably larger parcel of land Dad made available, a soon to become lifelong friend, Roger Fazendin, contracted to develop the property on appropriately sized lots. Dad provided us with seller financing that we repaid in three parts, and Roger Fazendin and Arnao-Plank split a substantially larger pot from which we personally extracted meaningful consideration. Years later, when Chuck resigned from Apache Oil Company, the forerunner to Apache Corporation, he was to prove quite successful in the construction and development of a number of apartment buildings.

"Get the philosophy right and the rest will quickly follow." Somehow I internalized that maxim early on, before Sally and I were married. And differences of philosophy can certainly create issues.

Frequently upon my return from the war I had discussed with Sally's mother, Ruth Bovey Stevens, the social changes I believed to be imperative for Americans, particularly affluent Americans, to comprehend, espouse, and live by. I liked and admired Ruth deeply, as well as loved her, but her worldview proved at odds with mine.

I felt that America was increasingly becoming a nation divided politically along the fault lines of haves against have-nots. My perception of the extremes of the basis for dissidence had been highlighted by awareness of the bitterness that accompanied the abject poverty during the Depression, contrasted sharply with near-regal lifestyles based on conspicuous consumption.

My experience in the military and among the poor of the Far East drove the point home with eye- and mind-opening clarity. In effect, for a few, too much had been given and too little was being asked. Our military had reflected men from all strata of education, economic and social status, caste, and color. In the postwar revitalization of our nation and its economy, I believed strongly that those of generational wealth should tread softly and go out of their way to adapt their own arrogant attitudes and social example, downsizing and humanizing both.

I knew I had been very fortunate in my own upbringing both with my family and the schools I had attended. I watched and respected people from both sides of the tracks. Frankly, decades later, I think Sal's mother grasped the discussions, yet when it came to her friends, children, or grandchildren her own privileged lifestyle and the status quo were too deeply ingrained. She couldn't grasp or espouse the changes I expected. I wanted the Plank children brought up differently and I needed understanding and cooperation. It was to become an endless tug-of-war, frustrating to all.

I would point to failed and failing lives among mutual acquaintances. These she could acknowledge, but she made no change in her personal approach. The Boveys and Stevens alike were more than generous with those to whom they saw it their responsibility to be helpful, kind, and generous. Perhaps Ruth's own mother better understood the important differences psychologically between checkbook diplomacy and personal direct involvement, for her outreach stretched deeply to those whose personal contact had become so meaningful. Sally understood it and was consistently more liberal than I, her involvement in seeking racial and women's equality extending well beyond the first phase of my own activism for extended human dignity.

I believed that the American dream of a better life due to effort, commitment, and example, and supported by personal sacrifices, contributed to personal growth and happiness. I believed that individuals were entitled to the fruits of their labors, including riches, assuming they were acquired through application of honest endeavor and fair play. I felt it a long-term threat, however, to America and the peoples on earth when those making an inordinate display of personal riches and privilege knew neither limits, restraint, nor the importance of reaching out, beyond themselves, to others where individual and private-sector initiatives could make an important difference.

An early indication that Ruth Stevens and I were not of complementary philosophies gave me a jolt on an otherwise perfect evening of celebration, as Sally and I happily shared our intention to marry. In an aside, when we were alone, Ruth smiled as she said, "Raymond, I do hope you will be able to support Sally in the manner to which she is accustomed." My immediate response was probably something to the effect that I would endeavor to do so. Inside, though, I was deeply troubled. I resolved to be able to provide more funds and personal effort to outreach than her net worth. Ruth's comment was not essential to my motivation.

Sally's and my first child and daughter, Katherine Bovey Plank, was born eighteen-plus months following our immense wedding and reception at Sally's family's estate, Hillsdale, in Ferndale, Wayzata, Minnesota. Kate, or "Kocky," as we were to nickname her, arrived two weeks ahead of schedule, a healthy, active, and (as newly arrived babies go in the eyes of their families) beautiful little girl. Her birth was well timed. By delivering on December 31, 1948, Sally won the $100 I'd kiddingly proffered as an early birth tax incentive. I happily and promptly remitted.

The pattern that had been established during Sally's and my long engagement gained momentum at the time of Kate's birth. Ruth, nicknamed "Ganny," had already seen our child by the point at which the nurse called me to the window to view her in the nursery before her return to her mother. "Isn't she beautiful?" Ganny asked, as she gave me a list of names of family to call and inform.

Husbands were not allowed to be present during childbirth in those days, a process which had been altered when my third wife, Heather, gave birth to her only child and my youngest son, Raby Plank, named for my father. That first night, Ganny, a director of the then all-woman board of the Northwestern Hospital, later to become Abbott Northwestern, spent the night in a private room near her daughter. Sally and I didn't see each other until she walked gingerly down the hall and was handed Kate, as the three of us returned to her room. We were alone together for a few minutes before the nurse politely told me it was after visiting hours and time for me to leave. Tired as I was after that important December 31, I remember thinking, "Now isn't that strange." I would see Sally and Kate en route to the office the next day and after work. I had made calls to Sally's and my friends, plus Grandma's list, and fell into bed in our recently completed home.

I was determined that our children be brought up, rather than in the "grand manner," with a minimum of its influence on their lives. Sal's mother's influence helped thwart my ability to balance their young lives' exposure, a balance that had been my fortunate lot. After her husband married a waitress from the Minneapolis Club, Ruth Stevens needed to bestow companionship and upbringing upon her brood of grandchildren. Unfortunately, we lived nearest to Ganny.

As Ruth's oldest child and only daughter, Sally received more than a full measure of attentive "help," Christmas and Easter holidays especially. Each grandchild, as well as their parents, was expected to give one another a Christmas present. The Christmas tree's lower limbs became engulfed with piles of beautifully wrapped and adorned packages, so numerous that Sally had to maintain the lists for subsequent thank-you notes. There were so many toys that the children wallowed in them, unable to sort and take them to their rooms, or to decide which would next get a few moments' focus. Sally and I did achieve partial success by establishing a family protocol that limited the exchange to one gift per family.

How much better it might have been had the Plank children been allowed to select and retain the half-dozen gifts they most wanted, and then delivering the rest to agencies serving children.

Easters were a delight for the children, yet a bane of my existence. For a week or more prior to Easter Sunday, eggs rolled into Ruth's home to be hard-boiled and tinted in colors that transcended the rainbow and possible faces on the moon. I would have preferred egg decoration and hunting in our own yard, but three of Ruth's sets of grandchildren lived within five miles of her command center. As the Easters and buckets of eggs rolled on, I boycotted the event.

Years later, I was shown a handsome memoir Ruth had written and distributed among her then family. One passage I found particularly fascinating, as the history offered a close view of not only the United States, but Russia and the world divided.

On May 26, 1896, Grandmother Bovey, as a small child, attended the coronation of Czar Nicholas II and Czarina Alexandra in Russia. The memoir noted days of preparation of suitable attire to properly participate in one of the last regal coronations. Within two decades of the coronation, the gulf between conspicuous wealth and abject poverty had led to the Russian Revolution and the assassination of the royal couple and their own young children. It is telling that Ruth reveled in the association with royalty and its excesses.

For my part, I saw the problems with the disparity between the haves and have-nots in the 1940s. In the decades since, I have come to comprehend much more about this gangrenous gap, and have sought to make a small difference through lighting candles of hope in support of youth and their essential mentors—teachers.

My five children at Christmas—Mike, Pamela, Dana, Kate, and Roger.

THE BIRTH OF APACHE

LITTLE DID I KNOW THAT what had started with accounting and tax work associated with Minneapolis oil investors—something I pursued as a long-term vehicle to grow Plank and Somekawa's accounting and tax practice—would lead to the formation of Apache Corporation.

In the early 1950s I had a clear perception of the importance to our government and the world's energy producers of replacing oil production diverted during World Wars I and II on behalf of our military forces and those of our allies. There had been little drilling in the United States during each of the wars, and our American resources were being rapidly depleted. Postwar, the search for more oil and gas would involve not only our producing states, but also globally. Our government was quick to "incentivize" the domestic search through tax incentives. Washington also committed to paying down our then immense war debts, which meant substantial increases in graduated income taxes; the top tax rate would exceed 90 percent of gross income following World War II, compared to 1 percent in 1916.

This combination of confiscatory tax rates on the one hand, and drilling and production tax incentives on the other, encouraged highly taxed individuals to invest in the search for oil and gas. Promoters, many functioning beyond the limits of scruples and integrity, quickly moved into likely areas around the country in pursuit of fortune. The oil boom swept beyond oil-producing states, and because many people's incomes (and taxes) were growing with the strong economic revival, oil and gas promoters found soft targets of opportunity in larger centers of population, including Minneapolis.

It did not take much time or brain power to expand Plank and Somekawa's accounting and tax services business through our contacts relevant to oil and gas: we provided oil and gas investor groups' accounting and tax services. We saw it as our responsibility to understand the basis for change and growth of our served market. To this end I did a lot of inquiring and learning, and when we recognized charges out of line with costs of drilling, completing wells, and acquiring and holding back acreage from investors, I checked directly with oilfield service providers.

With my trusty Minox camera (the size of a cigarette pack, it was the model carried by military intelligence personnel during the war), I personally uncovered kickback checks that were fattening the purses of unscrupulous promoters. I reported these findings to a group of investors, and their response was instant, vibrant, and unanimous: "You must take over and manage our assets." And these were substantial interests.

That, I knew, would require a great deal of thought, research, and planning before a decision could be made, for we knew nothing about either finding oil or completing and producing

In the early Apache days. I'm flanked by Truman Anderson and Chuck Arnao.

wells. I would need to develop a staffing plan, a budget, and funding for a small, dedicated business before submitting a proposal to manage and run an energy company. The proposal needed to encompass the basis for continuity, investment, and growth. We would also need to select a board of directors from among those who owned shares or who participated in drilling programs to which we had a fiduciary responsibility. That concept also held true when, in the early 1960s, it was apparent that the price of oil had fallen to a point where unless we developed alternative sources of income, we would not survive.

Approximately two months after agreeing to consider the proposal that we enter the program business, for which we did not feel qualified, we met with investors and their representatives. Fred Clifford, a tall, white-haired businessman, put his arm around me and said, "This is going to be a great opportunity for you, Raymond; we want you to go forward and repre-

*The first APA: Anderson, Plank & Arnao. We later
added the "che" at the suggestion of employee Helen Johnson.*

sent us and participate with us." The meeting included the legal counsel of a group of bilked investors. It was a huge moment!

Apache Corporation was accordingly founded in 1954 by Truman Anderson, Chuck Arnao, and yours truly.

In this phase I was greatly assisted by Fenelon Boesche, a senior Tulsa attorney knowledgeable in the oil business. (Bob Flanagan, a founder of one of the investor groups that had been ripped off, was careful to check Fenelon out very thoroughly prior to recommending him.) On paper, we designed a small company that called for equity investment of $250,000. Fenelon also recommended and referred me to geologist T. C. ("Ted") Bartling. Ted was attracted to the prospect of joining as cofounder an entity with strong relationships and able to attract investors. He had gained knowledge of tax incentives and knew some of the "oil patch warriors" who interacted with McBride Oil Company of St. Louis, operating from a base of single-family wealth.

In addition to the fact that we did not know each other beyond our favorable reputations—of the three Minneapolis partners, mine was considerably better known and recognized—there was a structural problem. Ted wanted a three-year

With Ted Bartling and George McLernon.

contract with his salary deposited in escrow. Furthermore, he wanted an equity stake equal to our own. I felt the three-year pay escrow inappropriate. We were able to work this out initially by consolidating our three Minneapolis operations, absent the escrow pay request. Apache would initially remain our selling arm, and we would work our way out of the assets and liabilities associated with our oil assets. We'd each be paid the same salary, and Ted would need to look at Apache's capitalization and his own oil-finding performance.

On January 25, 1955, we reached an agreement and Ted Bartling joined Apache. Ted wanted a capable geologist to become his first employee, and also hired a combined executive assistant, secretary, bookkeeper (obviously a very competent and appropriately paid woman to conduct all three functions), and a land man.

Ted's choice of geologist was John Woncik who, born poor, son of a coal miner, and reared in the east, had earned his degree in geology at the University of Minnesota. To this day I think of him as an oil-finding genius and a great teacher. He was also an outdoorsman, a hunter and fisherman; the trunk of his car invariably contained shotgun, shells, fishing rods, boots, a well-encased microscope, and rolled maps—and was conspicuously devoid of golf clubs.

It was important to the fledgling Apache that we remain in the hunt for oil in 1955. We had decided that our first full-year program would be in 1956, and that to this end we would transition in 1955, not with individual drilling prospects but with several at a time. In this way we would have product continuity for both our market and our sales force—obviously with competition from oil promoters, we needed product; obviously, too, a commission-based sales force would fall apart without product to sell.

Communications were important, both verbal and written. I serviced a large number of investors and handled written communications with customers and sales force during this period. Because we were in a startup phase of a publicly owned company, shareholder communications was the third leg on the communications stool. A diary entry from February 1955, notes that, following a weeklong trip to Tulsa, I wrote a twenty-four-page trip report, a practice I had developed as a base for targeted constituency communications.

All three of the Minneapolis partners individually and jointly worked through the problems of consolidation of our oil interests. One of these was a particularly sticky wicket. Sherrod and Apperson, an oil well promotional enterprise, was sliding down the financial hill, unable to pay for its contracted services and in danger of being unable to make cash distributions of oil

APACHE OIL CORPORATION
Statement of Income and Expense
For the Period from Inception (January, 1955) to December 31, 1955

INCOME

Gross profit on sale of properties	$18,389.54	
Lease bonus income	96,055.63	
Dry hole contributions received	43,341.96	
Gross profit from sale of turnkey drilling contracts	462.39	
Geological fees	27,156.10	
Oil and gas sales	2,580.96	
Interest income	2,315.87	
Miscellaneous	166.90	
Total Income		$190,469.35

EXPENSES

Geological department expenses	$46,322.79	
General and administrative expenses	42,190.62	
Depreciation and depletion	3,079.06	
Abandonment of leases, etc. considered worthless	73,272.55	
Dry hole expense	10,497.91	
Federal and State income taxes (Note 2)	2,571.17	
Total Expenses		177,934.10
Net Income for the Year		$ 12,535.25

The accompanying notes are an integral part of this statement.

From Apache Corporation's first annual report.

revenue to its investors.

A large, wealthy family group, whose prominence was influential to others, was represented by an able family lawyer, T. R. Andersen. While I took steps to get the industry service companies paid, T. R. found a group headed by an insurance mogul, the head of which ultimately created the MacArthur Foundation. MacArthur, in connection with founding and taking public an independent oil company, had the objective of rolling other oil assets into it. T. R. folded into it his Bell family clients, as well as those associated with us. We all took shares that were converted to cash in the initial offering. A close call—we breathed a sigh of relief.

With Joseph Kingman of First National Bank, Minneapolis.

Before Apache's formation, we had separately sold interests in a number of wells in the Cushing, Oklahoma area. Fenelon Boesche had proven very helpful in this arena as well, introducing us to a drilling contractor, Ben Novak, whose reputation and energy level were good. And so, on balance, were the prospects which we agreed to drill, in part because of the early advancement of technology in sand-fracking wells to increase production rates by improving the permeability and drainage areas beyond the well bores. (In many potentially productive oil reservoirs, the sandstone rock containing the oil may be too tight to yield oil in commercial quantities. By pumping sand through the pipe perforations under high pressures, pathways to the well bore are opened up, and some of the sand used to frack the well remains in the formation past which the oil flows en route to the pipe and surface. The result is that a larger percentage of the oil in place is recovered at higher rates, contributing to potential profit.)

Ben handled our well operations on a negotiated fee basis. We didn't have the internal capability to drill, which gave him an advantage, not unlike a number of drillers and operators at the time. While the investor results were attractive enough to enable the expansion of our investor base, and while his charges were competitive and reasonable, the potential for conflict was obviously one to deal with early in Apache's development.

For a period, we discussed and considered rolling Ben's operations into Apache for equity. Such consideration did not advance to the point of negotiating specific terms. Ben, who had become a friend, wanted to build his drilling business. The times were good, he thought, and his employees strong enough—those factors, coupled with available bank financing and his own care as an operator, meant he would best be served by remaining a driller.

On our side, we were not attracted to being in the drilling business for two important reasons. First and foremost, an inherent conflict of interest would exist between our program investors and our operations people. To us, drilling was a cost we must control, versus profit from. Second, in any basic commodity business, be it minerals, agriculture, real estate, or commercial banking, unbridled optimism could adorn the gravestones with chiseled lettering, following a short life span: "Here lies an optimist."

Ben did become overextended. Had he joined up, the chances are good that his stake could have grown to over a billion dollars. Ben was a competitive contractor. He had not retained interests in the wells he drilled for us, obviating one potential conflict at the outset. Although he added to his rig fleet, his operation could not drill competitively beyond the limited geographic areas that were his primary focus. The farther he moved away from his core, the more he needed to charge and the greater his competitive disadvantage.

From another early referral by Fenelon, we drilled several prospects generated by an eminent geologist, Russell Tarr, who found us several oil fields and was responsible for our drilling a prospect on an immense acreage block in Rio Arriba County, New Mexico. Unfortunately, our discovery was natural gas, at a time when gas had no market and fracking technology was in its infancy. Fifty years later, fracking was extensively applied throughout the Apache operations. Russell and Apache both realized that the formation of Apache spelled change. He preferred to develop a few quality prospects, while retaining an interest. We remained good friends.

I remember, and it has become a frequently plagiarized phrase at Apache, when I asked Russell, "How good is our latest discovery?" With a twinkle in his eyes he'd respond, "It's better than it is."

As I have always believed that our year-end reports to our program investors and shareowners should include reserves as determined or verified not by us but by independent firms of petroleum engineers, for many years we employed the Tulsa-based firm of Keplinger and Wanenmacher. (Fenelon had introduced

Sally and me with Conley and Marney Brooks on the New Amsterdam cruise.

me to Henry Keplinger, who became a friend and respected industry professional.) Independent petroleum engineers, in addition to their original value to us, serve other constructive purposes. Their reports are relevant to lenders, investment bankers, and independent accountants. Apache decided at the outset to utilize Arthur Andersen and Co. as accountants.

During early 1955, Sally and I had joined Conley and Marney Brooks on a ten-day cruise out of New York City on the New Amsterdam, a fabulous ship with great service, food, and our then favorite Bordeaux, Château Olivier 1947. Stopping at numerous ports of call, including Haiti, Panama, Colombia, and Havana, we shared many hours of conversation and developed relationships with other travelers.

Among the numerous topics we covered was an oil exploration business named Austral, headed by one Mr. Stewart, who tailored his refined English accent and his investor base to the country's super rich. That was a market, and therefore a program structure, that we did not approach because we did not access the narrow pinnacle of the super rich. Austral's multi-year structure afforded operational and thereby investment advantages. The company sought very large reserves and investors who recognized that it might be years before those reserves could be developed and brought to production. Austral did, however, register its programs with the Securities and Exchange Commission, and had a unique approach to reserve reporting. At the end of each year, the company issued three reserve reports; one internally developed and written, plus the reports of two outside firms.

That format had no appeal to us for several reasons: although Apache later had a very strong internal reserve engineering group, and while we employed a respected independent, middle-of-the-road engineering firm, we were sensitive to redundancy of costs. We reasoned that external appraisals would carry the most weight, including IRS reports relevant to estate, gift tax, or as in evaluation for sales or purchases. Nevertheless, Conley arranged for me to meet Mr. Stewart, whom I found to be a valuable contact.

In my diary entry of February 6, 1956, I noted that at the end of our second month of Apache operations, we had generated $33,000 in revenues and "added $16,000 to equity." While we were at the bottom of the recorded list of more than fifteen thousand upstream U.S. oil businesses, we had probably done more right than wrong, having thus far committed no fatal errors!

An organization is, and must be, dynamic versus static. Originally, in deciding who would be our first president, we relied on a coin toss. The toss, on the way to lunch, dismayed pedestrian sidewalk traffic, the more because three coins came up heads. I won the second toss, and subsequently concluded that I would retain that position due to my disproportionate contribution to the business, particularly in sales to customers.

The question of compensation was another matter. Chuck Arnao was performing services for several small operations, to which Anderson contributed nothing and I less than Chuck. While Chuck did a good job at these, and though he was active in Apache, he was not in the mainstream. He agreed to a $5,000 lesser compensation than Anderson, Bartling, or I were paid. In December 1956, however, an outside director close to Truman Anderson complained to me by phone that Chuck's Apache compensation was inappropriate, which led to a partner discussion and Chuck's withdrawal at the end of the year.

As our corporate names Plank, Anderson, Peet, Arnao, as well as Plank and Somekawa, suggest, when we founded Apache, two years earlier, we partners had more to work through than dropping our new business into the pond with other chirping frogs. We now needed to proceed in an orderly fashion and either wind down, consolidate, or sell the other enterprises, to be certain of avoiding conflicts of interest with the now two-year-old Apache, and to implement our agreed-to relationship with Ted Bartling.

Arnao Plank Inc. (API) was our selling arm, which served to attract qualified sales personnel, train, and compensate them. API was structured in such a way that, following sales training, our sales force was remunerated on a commission basis. While the partners also sold to customers, the 5 percent sales commission, although levied at progressively lower charges based on customers' volume of business done, were not paid out but utilized to grow and train the sales group, and to carry the legal and administrative costs of the complex as a whole.

We concluded, and Apache's board concurred, that all oil-related functions of API should be amalgamated through a merger with Apache. Here Chuck Arnao was at a disadvantage, because his duties applied less to sales and more to administration and residual functions as our other businesses were being dismembered. When the oil-related functions were merged with Apache, the partnership format became inappropriate, which Chuck recognized. Chuck resigned, leaving me as the continuing president, and Anderson as executive VP, later to become our first chairman (the company's CEO would remain undesignated for years). Our sales force was unhappy lest Anderson and Plank compete with them for clients, which I remedied by freezing those customer accounts I serviced, and referring the considerable inflow of new accounts to our increasingly effective and capable sales and service group.

TAX ADVANTAGING

APACHE NEEDED CAPITAL AND SOURCES of earnings to accommodate the growing business. Part of the compensation
recovered by Apache was in the form of a 5 percent override
on the leaseholds acquired by Apache for program exploration
and drilling under our evolving program format. It occurred
to me that Apache had at hand an exceptional investment vehicle for clients with substantial income in the highest income-
tax bracket (91 percent). Also, the revenues derived by Apache
through the sale of overrides were to become a primary source
of funding increasing inventories of acreage and the tubular
goods utilized in well completion, and in oil and gas gathering
systems between well heads and pipelines.

From the investors' perspective, here's how the override
worked to mutual advantage. Each drilling program would acquire and test a certain amount of acreage. Perhaps 80 percent
of the acreage allotted to an exploration program would be
found either nonproductive or noncommercial. That acreage
found could be abandoned and expensed for tax purposes by
the purchaser of the override and serve as a reduction of tax-

able income. The remaining 20 percent of the prospect acreage would generate revenues subject to depletion allowance, which then enabled up to 27.5 percent to be treated as a return of the invested capital and therefore not taxed.

Here's an example of how this could work: If a taxpayer bought one-half of a given program's override on all that year's leases, at a fixed price per acre totaling $200,000, he could expect to deduct 80 percent, or $160,000. His remaining after-tax cost would be $40,000 of nondeductible cost, plus 10 percent (were he in the 90 percent tax bracket) of the $160,000 deducted, or $16,000, for a total after-tax cost of $56,000.

The investor then had two choices. Assume that his original investment doubled, earning him an additional $200,000. The pre-tax return on the $56,000 of after-tax capital would be equal to three-plus times his investment. Of that $200,000, $55,000 would be a nontaxable 27.5 percent depletion allowance. He'd pay 90 percent of the remaining $145,000 in taxes. Alternatively, and based upon independent reserve appraisals, the present worth of his assumed revenue stream of $200,000 could be expected to approximate two-thirds, or $167,000, of future tax savings. This royalty stream he could donate to charity or give as gifts to children or grandchildren.

In reality, the purchasers of the overrides did, on average, a great deal better than what I describe above. Some wealthy investors, rather than give the overriding royalties to charity, had children or grandchildren in lower tax brackets. The high-bracket investors, working with their tax and estate-planning attorneys, might in some instances give the assets to lower-tax-bracket heirs relatively early in the periods of the production when valuations had not yet peaked, thus further minimizing income, gift, and estate tax considerations.

During Apache's important early years, the company received several million dollars at a particularly important survival and growth period. Because the majority of Apache investors' benefits from our drilling programs were deferred until leases paid out, and the override sales were deductible in large part by our investors, we held much of the acreage we acquired and did not assign it to our drilling programs. Accordingly, a small portion of the income generated became taxable; most of it offset costs incurred yet not recovered from our programs. Eventually Apache phased out the 5 percent overrides for competitive reasons, but they had proved their utility.

Gradual changes in tax rates reduced the appeal of oil investments through the 1960s and early 1970s. However, because Apache was managing the investment and tax interests of our investors, assisted by legal and tax attorneys, those we served well rewarded us with confidence and referrals of more business. Those promoters who limited their interest to "the deal" were at an increasing competitive disadvantage. Once able to amalgamate these functions under the Apache roof, we found attendant advantages.

As Apache grew, so did our insatiable need for working capital and for liquidity in the market for our shares. The first innovation occurred relatively early in our corporate life. With due regard to compliance with federal and state regulations, for every $15,000 program unit we sold, we offered the buyer the option to acquire two hundred shares of Apache stock at the market price at the time of the per-unit purchase.

My rationale, which proved popular, was based on two primary points. If the program investor wanted to maintain an equity interest in the company related to the size of his program investment, the options received at the time of his unit purchase would help the early bird investor preserve his equity ratio in the company. Further, because his unit purchase generated a call on the growth of Apache, which correlated to the success of our programs, the unit purchaser had the benefit of a possible source of long-term capital gains income, taxable at lower rates than gains generated on the program drilling side. This feature was appealing to numerous executives, and spread to others, helping our sales efforts. It gave our sales force more to talk about, while attracting interest to our shares as well.

While the override royalty approach was my idea, a further innovation that we developed into a fine art was contributed by our top salesman, Robert Olson, who for years was affectionately referred to as "the King" by our admiring sales force and some of his personal clients. Bob had been an accountant with Plank and Somekawa.

Bob, with the collaboration of three other Minneapolis-based salesmen, coined the idea of "double bracketing." It was designed to appeal to high-earning professionals whose earned income could be expected to drop substantially upon their retirement, and with it, their tax brackets. Why not suggest, Bob reasoned, that the clients invest annually during the high-income years, and reduce the level of annual investment as they retired? Early investment and development of holdings would take place at high deductibility, and cash return would be maximized later in the cycle when the retiree was in a lower bracket.

The sales force developed bell curves to illustrate the principle, as well as to provide a basis for modeling their net deductions of unit-generated net revenues. This approach added to the quality of the service we provided, underscoring the value of planning over time, versus speculating on a given year's program performance. The average size of annual participations rose, and enhanced our competitiveness in an environment in which many copied our program approach.

While we were augmenting the services offered through our sales force, I recognized we had another category of investors. This consisted of high net-worth individuals and family-owned corporations whose retirement income was unlikely to decline. To some of these, already concerned with estate and gift taxes, the liquidity of the investments was a key consideration. The sale of their oil holdings was not particularly attractive for two reasons. First, their tax basis in the mature holdings was very low. They had very small after-tax cost basis because their tax incentives associated with their investments were efficient, leaving them with significant taxes to pay at the time of sale. Second, if we were to repurchase their holdings, Apache might benefit more than they would as sellers. Even with third-party appraisals this could represent a conflict of interest.

We developed an approach that more effectively addressed many investors' desires for liquidity, through a plausible exit strategy: the exchange of program interests for Apache shares. This way we could provide both third-party engineering evaluations and investment bankers' opinions that the exchange ratios for properties were fair. These valuations did not require a reduction in the value of the offer, because Apache already managed the assets. Nor did they require a repurchase outlay by Apache, which was able to conserve capital to fund growth.

The exchanging unit investors got a tax-free exchange into shares that deferred their income taxes until they sold the shares at long-term capital gains rates—lower than the rate at which their unit values would be taxed. Alternatively, they would possess a low after-tax-cost, highly liquid asset that they could use to optimum advantage to fund their charitable donation objectives. Or, if they had developed tax losses from the sales of other securities, they could offset the taxable gains they realized when they sold low basis Apache shares.

From Apache's perspective as a growth company, the build-up of critical mass through merging in units represented by properties we knew and operated provided "win-win" advantages to our program investors and Apache alike. Over the decades, Apache utilized variations of the tax-deferral format on a number of occasions. It was important to me that, rather than squeeze out unit investors, they be provided the alternative of retaining their holdings.

Through our program history, the majority of the potential innovations we considered came to naught. Some that we liked, we banked and they became available when the conditions, generally those of timing, became appropriate. Meanwhile, as the lives of our senior investors advanced, their needs changed, as did IRS requirements.

CHANGES DOMESTIC AND COMMERICAL

THE BIRTH OF OUR FIRST child, daughter Kate, was followed by our first son, Michael Raby, on May 12, 1951, eighteen months later. I was so excited with the girl-boy count that I hugged and kissed Dr. Haugen on the cheek as he emerged from the delivery room—apparently not a customary response. I recall his somewhat embarrassed expression before he fully reciprocated and joined in the celebration.

Mike was followed in due course by our exuberant daughter, Pamela. By 1955, the splendid little Cape Cod house into which Sally and I, with the help of Chuck Arnao, had poured so much of our energy, was bulging at the seams. Furthermore, as Sally wanted five children and I three (I fortunately lost that chapter in family planning), we set upon selecting a site, an architect, and the joys of planning ahead for our ultimate home together.

By the time Sally and I divorced, we had added two more boys to the family, Roger and Dana, and our campus included a pool in which all swam like fish, and a splendid tennis court. The kids were great and fun, though my narrower and firmer view on work ethic and values occasionally triggered dis-

Sally with our children.

sension. Quality time together at home was limited largely to tossing balls, swimming, picnics, and weekend jaunts to Lake of the Woods, 395 miles due north in Ontario, Canada. It was there that Mike caught his first fish, a 3-pound walleye pike. The proud boy noted, "Well, I've done that. Let's go in."

Our first home had been about 50 feet off Ferndale Road, which connected two main arteries to and from Minneapolis. Our replacement Shangri-La was on a wooded knoll far more remote—and lovely. There, neither the kids nor our dogs were at risk of being run over, a fate to which all three of our previous dogs had succumbed when a speeding garbage truck obliterated them en masse. The new house was several hundred yards from my aging parents, who on warm autumn days would sit outside and await the elder three as they exited the school bus and passed by the home of Grandpa Raby and Grandma Margie. The business proceeded at a seemingly slow gait, despite frenetic activity, matched at home by Sally's heavy schedule of children, social and business entertainment, and travel in both categories.

122

Cleaning fish at Lake of the Woods.

After an intermission, our brood was finally complete with the arrival of two more sons, Roger Barton, and Dana Raymond. I'm thankful that Sally won the family planning battle, for the youngest boys became great additions to my world, now filled with adult grandchildren and, as of 2012, seven great-grandchildren.

At least during their younger years, Sally's and my five children had quality time together on vacations in Europe and summer weekends on Lake of the Woods in Ontario, until the girls commenced dating.

For approximately ten years, I owned and personally restored a home on postcard-sized Lake Henry, 45 miles west of our Wayzata home. While small, Lake Henry did offer clear water. We bought a small pontoon boat with a canopy for $450 and a 3.5 horsepower Johnson motor for $125. On summer weekends, my two daughters would cling to the pontoons and squeal as we cut slowly through the water. Anchored on still evenings, we'd grill hamburgers on board until the mosquitoes buzzed us like kamikazes. It was on the country roads near Lake Henry that I taught my eldest daughter, Kocky, how to drive, park, back up, and make her way on snow and on icy winter roads. Here, too, Roger, Mike, and I planted evergreens and practiced shooting with .22 caliber rifles and shotguns. We fished, we painted the big old house, and Kocky rode her horse.

I purchased a small airplane and the Plank family world changed, bringing Mexico and the Bahamas into easy range. The three older children could accompany us on multiple trips as the travel time shrunk by two-thirds. Sally obtained her pilot's license and made use of her new skills. Later, son Roger obtained his pilot's license as well.

In that era I appropriated to personal use the motto, "Never confuse motion with action," which has served the company well in obtaining data, evaluation, risk assessment, and decision making.

When we founded Apache, my knowledge of the technical aspects of the oil and gas business was virtually nonexistent, while my financial and tax-related savoir faire may have had few competitive peers. Much of our travel to Tulsa (on frequent trips of seven to ten days), I spent developing a working knowledge of geology, well drilling, completions, engineering, and field operations.

Ted Bartling was a good teacher; his mentoring, however, was appropriately focused on the staff geologists working with our drilling and operations head, George McLernon. My knowledge base, still limited, was initially derived primarily from John Woncik, our fabulous teacher and oil finder; Harry Perry, a very able geologist; and John Black, a younger man who as a summer intern found us two commercial fields while majoring in geology at the University of Tulsa. These men were individually my companions on field visits while geology and engineering filled our conversations as Ted Bartling held prospect office reviews. Fortunately, too, all our key people enjoyed Lake of the Woods outings and endless business discussion. I was learning more by osmosis and interest; formality was dialogue versus mandate.

Organizationally, we allowed none of our personnel to acquire or own interests in oil properties, thus avoiding conflicts of interest. In the instance of prospecting and developing geologists and land men, practices varied. Most consultants of the era sought to develop a base of producing properties, and as such, would offer, for example, three-quarters of a play while retaining a cash-carried quarter interest. If Ted Bartling valued the prospect as much or more than self-generated prospects, he would take the plays and our programs would drill them.

Meanwhile, a schism began to widen between Truman Anderson and myself. The arguments between us became louder, and our small Minneapolis staff would cower as we threw a wastebasket or smashed an ashtray. The differences between Truman and me ran deep. He had grown up in a small-town environment in Wisconsin and had risen rapidly while selling life insurance in Minneapolis, where his contacts, both business and social, were more limited. I had the benefit of a private or independent school upbringing and education both at Blake and my war-interrupted Yale years. My business and social exposure from starting several businesses was from both sides of the tracks, and my early postwar acceptance was broad in Minneapolis and beyond.

My contacts were growing exponentially; Truman's, at a slower pace. I added to my contact base by civic involvement

John Woncik.

on multiple fronts, boards of directors, colleges throughout the state, and the University of Minnesota. Truman's contacts came largely through the One Two Club, plus the Air National Guard, in which he was a captain without combat or overseas duty. Truman was, however, building his base with a growing coterie of program investors, many of whom originally had come to us through my close personal friendship with Jack Cornelius, a senior giant within the ad agency BBD&O. Jack sourced our Iowa program prospects and shored the Apache base with the Merediths of Meredith Publishing Company and the Maytags of the original washer/dryer and later Maytag cheese business (the next generation of which took a turn at the wheel of the commercial air carrier business with Braniff Airlines).

George McLernon and Truman Anderson.

Truman and I differed on a more fundamental basis. My time horizons for Apache were long term; Truman was impatient in his personal drive to become a high roller. His monetary appetite was insatiable and he wanted the social acceptance to go with it. He came to regard me as the chief impediment to his aspirations. At first I did not fully understand the basis for these conflicts, yet as the years passed, John Kocur, who joined us from the east in 1969 as general counsel, made clear to me that "values are not created equal." I wanted to build the business; Truman wanted to build his personal fortune and fame. The conflict was basic.

Had I better understood the depth of our divergences, I would have managed the conflicts better. As it happened, Truman and I realigned our functions and I recommended to the board that he become chairman without naming either of us chief executive officer. Presiding at meetings—taking on the responsibility for board communications—he assumed direct control of our ambitious but amateurish foray into the ownership of three major office buildings, two in Minneapolis, including the tallest Minnesota building, Foshay Tower, plus the Rand Tower. He hired two experienced commercial realtors, one over buildings and one to lead the leasing and construction of the Apache Plaza, one of America's first enclosed malls. These added outreaches and attendant challenges kept him busy, but as shopping center lease rentals lagged behind forecasts, red ink began to mount, and with it, our détente lapsed into further discord.

Federal income tax rates had been reduced concurrently with decreases in daily allowables (mandated maximum outputs) of oil production in Oklahoma and Texas. I was deeply concerned that real estate spending overruns and a revenue shortfall required Apache capital at the same time that cash flow in our mainstay oil business was shrinking.

Truman, in the meantime, had consolidated his power authority by requesting and being granted the title of CEO. Finally his game plan became crystal clear to me. Given the impediments to our oil and gas business growth, in addition to running the financial side I had been busy developing the base of diversified smaller business units. I was at risk of being sidelined.

The theory behind the diversification was predicated upon the reality that Apache was a publicly traded entity; there were profitable and growing small businesses run by successful entre-

John Kocur.

preneurs, many of whom were unhappy with the prospect of being required by lenders to guarantee debt for expansion by accepting personal liability that frequently extended to one's spouse as well. Also, from the potential sellers' perspective, many had financial partners who had been content during the earlier growth of the enterprises, but now were ready to cash out. From experience gained as a member of the Young Presidents' Organization, as well as from board memberships on smaller companies, and our own practice of retaining financial authority, while delegating operations to capable, motivated individuals, an operations style and approach had emerged.

An example will serve to illustrate. One YPO self-made businessman had sold out to Motorola, which promptly swarmed operations with the headquarters' personnel and requirements plus a markedly higher corporate overhead. The previous owner repurchased the business, providing the equity to the next generation's avoiding gift taxes, while the father took preferred shares for cash he advanced in the repurchase. The business bounced back to greater profitability than ever. By then, John Kocur, who had joined the business on February 19, 1969, understood the message.

In the purchase of Goettl Brothers, we acquired the equity, getting Bill Goettl and his wife out of debt, while holding operations and financial planning reviews quarterly but not swarming Bill's business with smart-alec whiz kids armed with case studies to guide their opinions and ruin the business. When we acquired the business, a dominant air-conditioning and heating manufacturer marketer in the growing Southwest, its sales were at the annual level of $10 million. When we sold it within a decade, the revenues were $30 million, profits more than proportionately higher. Bill Goettl who had wanted to retire, turned over the reins to the purchaser, and Apache banked the equity growth. This process was oft repeated in years after we had swallowed our lumps taken in real estate.

Seneca Steel had been acquired while doing under $10 million in revenues, and though it provided a litany of near horrors following the death of the able and honest Harry Kurzman, Seneca reached $50 million in sales before the new president and sales manager colluded, for a time, in undetected kickbacks.

John Kocur spent a decade identifying the primary culprits profiting from collaborating from outside Seneca in the looting. John recovered $14 million in negotiated settlements, which were added to the proceeds a decade after we sold the business (at a bargain to a purchaser who turned it around). One of the Seneca culprits drew a multiyear hard prison sentence; the other was found in his apartment dead of questionable and undetermined causes, following which an autopsy was mysteriously not performed.

While seeking to rid Apache of me following the Seneca de-bacle, Apache's board required the departure of Truman An-derson, who made a Watergate-type blunder. After he was or-dered to give up the chairmanship he bugged our offices and our board and conference room. The bugs were found, the buggers fled, and finding our outside general counsel—an An-derson ally—out of town, I turned to Henry Halladay of the well-known and respected Dorsey firm. Halladay was assisted by Mike Wright, who later became the successful CEO of Su-perValu, a major regional force in grocery wholesaling.

Truman had been seeking to rally investors and support for a hostile takeover. He felt the ax blow from his bugging and spying on his associates, who signed a petition asking the board to fire him rather than me, which latter expedient Truman had proposed to the board. The vote was six to three in my favor. One of these conspirators, a fellow officer and senior finance vice president, I called to my office. Advising him that a basis for trust no longer remained, he could accept demotion, a pay cut, or get lost. He chose the latter (in a resignation letter to the board in 1964), and left to run a small oil company owned by a New York City family. His tenure there was short, and he then moved on to work with a minor Colorado savings and loan.

Lesson? Ego, important to self-acceptance and motivation, can quickly outstrip one's competence and the support of any organization that detects arrogance. Fat heads get flattened.

While it was "back to work" at Apache, we had a few things to attend to in reconstituting governance. I asked Charlie Swe-att, brother of the CEO and founder of Honeywell, to serve as chairman of the board, an invitation he accepted, recogniz-ing that his prominence and experience within the community

Charlie Sweatt, chairman of Apache Corp.

would be salutary to the riled Apache waters both within and outside the company. Charlie Sweatt's son, also Charlie, once came up to me on a social occasion and observed how great it was that Apache's little business attracted the time and focus of his father. He told me, "His involvement with that little company is good for him and keeps him out of the gardener's hair." What do you say when you'd like to say, "F— you?" Nothing, but you remember. It was a great line.

He made an excellent contribution for a number of years. Charlie Sweatt proved a first-rate chairman, running our meetings efficiently and obtaining the views of all members on policy matters. His wry humor and quick mind focused on Apache's and our investors' interests; he was exemplary. The contribution was splendid both inside and outside the company. Internally, he was particularly highly respected; both his manner and the

With my trusty pipe.

age separation endeared him to our younger chargers. At able director Malcolm Mackay's suggestion, endorsed by the full board, I invited Mike Belzer, a longtime friend of Truman's, to join the board. Mike made a splendid addition.

We had one outside detractor who owned the investigating firm that had bugged our offices. I had a frank one-on-one discussion with him in which he agreed that enough was enough, and we became better friends for the discussion. His son and successor at one point asked me if I might be interested in serving on the board of their insurance company, an offer I declined.

For a period of several months, I wrote a daily report of my activities that contributed to the basis for confidence and support from the board and was a practice well worth maintain-

I kept competitors' annual reports on the wall behind my desk. the better to study them.

ing between board meetings. (Even in 2004 I produced eighteen written updates, the better to foster directors' familiarity with dynamic Apache so as to render informed decisions at our meetings: among them timing the move from a mini-conglomerate back to oil and gas.)

As for Truman Anderson, he started a privately financed car wash business that though adequately funded, quickly fell from grace. He went broke and disappeared from the area, selling his fortress-like estate and moving with a new wife to Denver, then California. He put together oil deals, bringing a son into the business—it sank. Truman had a heart attack and died. I "missed" his funeral.

LAKE HENRY AND FLYING TIME

MALCOLM "BUD" MACKAY WAS A friend and a catalyst for a variety of ventures. Bud grew up in New Jersey, son of the senior partner of Laidlaw and Company, a venerable name in investment banking in eastern circles. With a love for the West resembling that of Teddy Roosevelt's, Bud's father had aquired a magnificent mountain and wheat ranch near Roscoe, Montana. Perhaps Bud's father drove his stake into the ground with greater deliberation and foresight than TR, for it truly was a great property and enduring asset.

At a tender age, young Bud took up flying, and became a pilot in his teens. His father died when he was but seventeen, and to him fell the chore of running Laidlaw during the Great Depression. Bud recalled his first day in charge, laden with the burden of firing over half of the staff, both elderly employees and green youths who had not been "pulling on the wagon." Bud held the downsized business together in part by flying his small plane from town to town, visiting commercial banks with trust departments. By fortifying himself as best he could with knowledge of their bond and equity holdings before calling on the presidents, he was able to show how they might restructure their holdings. This led to his firm's capturing the commission business, no small part of which was apparently selling the holdings in an entity from the trust department to the bank, and among other banks in the area. Bud's firm survived.

But World War II was imminent, and Bud was quick to serve his country by becoming a pilot in the Marines. The majority of his overseas duty was spent flying transports in the South Pacific. Dauntless, he rose rapidly in rank to become a colonel whose duties included flying the world-famous Charles Lindbergh on an extended trip around the Pacific theater.

He also saw plenty of Japanese and associated danger. In one instance, he flew a load of supplies to American troops pinned down on the shores of Hollandia. He came in high over the Japanese troops and landed downhill, a practice not uncommon among a number of us. Ground troops unloaded the cargo plane in jig time, warning him that the Japanese had advanced to the far end of the runway. Bud remained until the plane had been emptied, turned uphill, and flew directly at the firing enemy troops. He came away from the experience with holes in his plane but with his life—and another medal.

When Bud returned from the war, he became convinced that the heyday of commercial aviation was shortly ahead, and after selling his investment banking company, he invested heavily in Northwest Orient Airlines, believing its air routes to have good prospects. As airline stocks were then cheap, he and his family found themselves owning the largest block of Northwest Airlines stock ahead of the postwar explosion in passenger, mail, and freight cargoes.

Bud pulled up from New Jersey and moved with his lovely wife, Gray, to Minneapolis. The airport became Northwest's headquarters and the company was the soundest and best run airline for a number of years.

When I made my first cold call on Malcom Mackay, then executive VP, I took an immediate liking to him. He sat behind a medium-size desk of gray metal in an office where three seated guests on metal chairs would have been a crowd. Those chairs rested on a linoleum floor. No show here: Northwest was moving and holding its costs down. Bud Mackay was friendly, soft spoken, and candid, while quick to comprehend the key points of my informal presentation. No pretension here either—he was to become an outstanding director and mentor.

Northwest, which became a top airline, had a difficult time getting beyond blazing a trail. Its then president, Croil Hunter, was well liked and known for his spirited vision, but not for his pragmatism. Nonetheless, he had founded that airline that was to become a major air carrier and nurtured it through its early and difficult days.

An air force general seemed a good choice as a successor to Hunter. I recall at the time that the general appeared to believe he was indeed running the air force rather than a struggling commercial airline. His tenure was suitably limited, and Bud Mackay was credited with finding and retaining Donald Nyrop to become a highly respected CEO, who turned the carrier around and flew it forward.

When I first met Bud, my objective was to make him an Apache customer by selling him a program unit, and to sound him out on the possibility of becoming an Apache outside director representing program investors and shareowners. Within days he decided favorably on both counts, beginning a relationship that was to spur our program sales in New York City. He fostered many valuable relationships over the decades prior to his retirement as an Apache director and from our executive committee at the age of eighty.

Bud Mackay had acquired several farms along lakes within 75 miles of Minneapolis, believing that land on water closer to the Twin Cities of Minneapolis and St. Paul afforded excellent appreciation potential.

Liking Bud's approach, I decided to look around, contacting his rural land realtor. Within a month, he had found Lake Henry and a 113-acre farm located on a small but deep-water lake about an hour's drive from downtown Minneapolis. On the property was a large home in need of paint, a barn for cattle and horses, a large corn crib, a storage shed, and a rickety narrow dock. It included a 20-acre hardwood forest. The purchase price was $19,000, with almost a mile of shoreline. Apache benefit? Some: hosting business contemporaries on weekends and two annual company summer picnics complete with swimming, horseshoes, and a high swing into the water. But mainly, Lake Henry became a family place.

When the kids reached dating age, Lake Henry lost its luster for them. I found myself driving up alone on weekends to cut the grass, cover the first and second floor walls with knotty cedar, and remodel the second floor into bedroom space that was infrequently used. For several years I leased out the fields, thus defraying a portion of the costs.

I loved the place, often taking my briefcase and working out of it after dark over short weekends. When I sold the farm ten years after I'd bought it, it brought in $55,000, more than double my sunk cost. I would guess that in twenty more years the acreage on the beautiful deep-water lake would have brought $500,000 to $1 million or more. Bud Mackay had been right—land on water within easy range of the Twin Cities was an excellent investment.

When Northwest Airlines moved its headquarters to Twin Cities International Airport, Bud became a neighbor at Long Lake, Minnesota, buying a large old home from David McLaughlin, president of Toro, the lawnmower and snowblower company. Bud would drop by the office after downtown luncheons at the Minneapolis Club, and we saw more of each other with our houses only three miles apart.

We began to discuss private flying, which I had given up seventeen years previously, following the war. He asked me if I didn't miss flying, and I allowed that I did.

"Then why don't you buy a Cessna 175 like mine? I hangar it with Art Ryan at Flying Cloud airport, a half-hour from your house and equidistant from your office."

I agreed to meet Art Ryan with Bud one afternoon; Ryan had a new Cessna 175 in stock, which I bought that afternoon for $17,500. Ryan took me around the field and landed, and we traded seats. I took off, flew the traffic pattern, and landed it, seventeen years without flight time melting like an ice cube dropped into hot soup. When I reached home, I said to Sally, "Guess what I did this afternoon?" The family was enthusiastic. Sally and Roger went on to obtain their pilot's licenses. Getting the plane was a life-changing event.

I frequently flew the Cessna on business to Tulsa, Dallas, Louisiana, Houston, Calgary, and Chicago. My arrangement with Apache was that I would charge the company the equivalent commercial airfare, or for cities not conveniently served, the car mileage reimbursement. On quasi-personal and business flights to Lake of the Woods, our employees were frequent passengers from Tulsa, along with plant and operations managers from Buffalo and from Fresno and Stockton, where we made plastic pipe.

In my time as campaign finance manager (for a gubernato-

My sons Mike, Dana, and Roger with the Cessna.

rial and a couple of congressional campaigns), I could hit up to four cities a day in the Cessna. For the YPO Education Committee, I flew to the state's eleven college towns to speak to the students. On compressed personal vacation trips, the plane facilitated repeat trips to Mexico City, the Bahamas, Phoenix, and Lake Tahoe—as well as hunting and fishing trips to the Dakotas, Canada, and Bud Mackay's marvelous Montana ranch.

The trusty Cessna 175 gave way to its successor, a second-hand Cessna 310, followed by a new Cessna 337, a high-wing "push-pull" twin engine with cabin oxygen and swift 190 mph ground speed. When I gave up piloting, I had logged, including my air corps training and combat, 3,500 pilot hours.

Roger and Dana on a drilling rig.

RECLUSE PETROLEUM
AND FOUNDING UCROSS

ON A SUMMER FRIDAY IN 1966, I was en route to a weekend with a program-investing couple at their summer residence on Lake Tahoe. My route took me over the Powder River Basin of Wyoming, a significant oil-producing basin east of the Rockies.

I had long been aware of the importance of the east side of the "Powder" and of Campbell County, Wyoming, as a major source of oil at the time, making it fifth in oil production behind Texas, Louisiana, Oklahoma, and California. I was well aware of the large Muddy Sandstone discovery at the north end of the basin in Montana. Shell had discovered a deep field on the western side of the basin. One of my checkpoints en route west was Reno, Wyoming, near the location of Shell's deep but relatively small field. As I flew on to the west, I began to think there must also be oil on the west side, as well as in the northern reaches of the basin. On landing for gas, I called John Woncik in Tulsa, who was eager to map and explore the area.

Recluse, which we began to drill in July 1967, was to become Apache's largest find up to that point. Wyoming wells had no oil allowables, enabling us to produce at rates of three hundred

Recluse Petroleum Club.

to one thousand barrels per day. Even though the high-gravity crude sold for but $3 per barrel, the field reinvigorated our drilling program business. The prolific flows from Recluse came at a critical period before prices advanced sharply in the '70s—and then tanked again in the '80s.

Apache's discovery opened a new area to exploration, and we and our competitors were quick to follow up with a series of discoveries of commercial fields in the Powder River Basin. The Recluse discovery led to a complementary series of business initiatives that made a difference not only within the state, but beyond.

Because we would be visiting Recluse, I bought a small cattle and hay ranch on a mile and a half of stream fed by the snow melt and rains in the Big Horn Mountains. This led in turn to assembling a group of twenty-one families whose purpose it was to acquire other ranches in close proximity and to shape

The Recluse Discovery Well.

them into an economic unit of critical mass, allowing us to restore buildings and expand irrigation. Connecting one large ranch house with a staffed guesthouse, the unit also became a center for the partnership families to bring their children to experience the west.

Having driven the 790 miles from Minnesota to Buffalo, Wyoming, and having flown over the fields, streams, and the varying terrain, a central thought struck me. Many of the buildings from the 1880s to 1920s were abandoned to the weather, harsh winds, and collapse. While all were part of a passing era, some were particularly representative of their heyday, too well-constructed to allow them to be destroyed by rain. Part of our ranch group's objective became the restoration and preservation of these structures, as well as finding a use for them in the century beyond their construction.

We decided to build a small conference center and artists-in-

Big Red at the Ucross Foundation.

residence program. The restoration extended into a decade long series of projects, built around the Ucross Foundation which I founded in 1981. By the time the twenty-fifth anniversary of the Ucross Foundation was celebrated in 2006, more than one thousand writers, visual artists, choreographers and composers had enjoyed Ucross residencies. Many found themselves inspired by the land and environment to realize more of their human and artistic potential. Ucross clearly has fostered happiness and success by providing creative people their quality time, commitments, and the environment. Five Pulitzer Prize winners, five MacArthur Foundation "genius" grants, National Book Awards, Tony Awards and a host of other honors that have stemmed from Ucross residencies attest to validity of the concept, which is alive and vital in 2012.

REAL ESTATE
AND DIVERSIFICATION

THE DECADE OF THE '60s, which encompassed a wide-ranging mixture of initiatives, also found me having to deal with the consequences of expansion, including serious people problems. The most poignant of our Apache failures was in commercial real estate. Truman Anderson and I were breaking ground new for both of us. To Truman, this venture looked easy, which I truly believe he thought it would be. In hindsight, I believe the greatest liability that he brought to the real estate business was his oversized ego.

As we looked at real estate operations in Minnesota and around the United States, the successes were more apparent than the failures. It appeared easy enough to Truman to recruit competent building management and hire construction oversight to manage venerable old office buildings, construct shopping centers, and lease shopping centers to the professionals.

But unlike our careful approach in oil, in real estate we omitted the important step of learning the business. For Apache, real estate success was not to be. Perhaps the two competing vice presidents who reported to Truman might have spared Apache some of our costly errors had Truman Anderson developed the basic knowledge essential to analyze and guide his staff. He could have learned the business by studying the models of successful operators instead of relying on the perceptions of the conflicted real estate brokers and our outside counsel, who profited handsomely even as we wasted money.

It is difficult enough in any startup mode to learn while doing and at the same time provide sound guidance to one's senior subordinates. When one contrasts Apache's real estate failure with our successful oil program business, the contrasts help illuminate both omissions and commissions.

The strengths of Apache en route to growth and substance in our primary field of endeavor were instructive templates. Starting with a long-range set of objectives for our enterprise, we built on a knowledge base that gave us a competitive edge as well as financial muscle on which to predicate, identify, and support technical competence. Ted Bartling had both the technical background and the operations experience and ability to find oil and gas to support our tax-incentivized and sophisticated program innovations. He also hired and gave hands-on guidance to capable men who became expert both within Apache and beyond, when they went out on their own.

A fundamental difference, however, between Truman Anderson and myself, was that I knew what I did not know and the extent to which I had to learn to "walk the talk" more than "talk the walk." Stated another way, it's easier to promote on a short-term basis than to build incrementally, a step at a time, to last.

In the late-1950s, when Oklahoma and Texas oil allowables were cut by up to 90 percent, so were our revenues; our lifeline was threatened and real estate, our weakest point, became our

Apache Realty groundbreaking for the Apache Mall in Rochester, Minnesota.

greatest exposure. Some might have walked from our commitments. I didn't think that honorable, or worth consideration. We had to make the most of it while facing the worst of it.

Our offensive strategy was to pivot away from real estate and acquire, in exchange for shares of our stock, successful, entrepreneurially driven businesses which would grow. My objective was to find revenues enabling us to bridge the gap occasioned by the twin adversities associated with our losses in real estate and the cyclical downturn in the oil and gas business. Defensively, we pursued as orderly a withdrawal from real estate as possible, selling off the assets encumbered by specific related debt.

First to go was the Bankers Building, an aged, historic, but outmoded office building in Milwaukee, which itself was no

The Foshay Tower.

paragon of growth. Milwaukee suffered as the beer business hastened its consolidation—Anheuser-Busch emerged as a world powerhouse, beating out Milwaukee brands Pabst, Blatz, Old Milwaukee as well as Minnesota's Hamm's and Gluek's.

In Minneapolis, Wheelock Whitney of Dain Kalman & Quail acquired the splendidly constructed Rand Tower from us. They made major renovations, then tied it into the advancing skyway system, which was cooled for the summer season and warmed for Minnesota's frigid and snowy winters. This enabled second-floor rentals and small service businesses to serve downtown office employees. These modifications suited the vibrant city's growing national and international businesses.

The Foshay Tower, which we had acquired and occupied, had a fascinating history and evolution in itself. Named by Wilbur Foshay for himself, this tower was long the tallest building west of the Mississippi. For years, the Foshay Tower enjoyed two unique revenue sources. The first was a balcony around its top, to which both locals and visitors from hundreds of miles took the elevator to gaze out upon the surrounding city of lakes. "The balcony" was a frequent stop for school groups and visitors in town for major league football, baseball, and basketball games. The quarter admission fees piled up for a long time, only to fade as the views were cut off by Foshay's new taller neighbors. The second low-cost revenue source was from the then growing forest of antennae for radio and television transmission attached to the tower. This, too, was a temporary attribute.

In the Foshay block was the headquarters of the area's largest, and most prominent S&L, Twin Cities Federal Savings and Loan. Twin Cities developed a plan to consolidate our shared block, allowed Apache to sell them the Foshay Tower, and thus Apache completed its Dunkirk-like withdrawal from office buildings.

In Apache's subsequent diversification we did more things right than wrong. Not only were we able to grow cash flow and profitability, but ego and stupidity did not bring us down. In the businesses we acquired, we avoided the major error of the era's conglomerates. Many of those, upon acquiring smaller businesses, too frequently superimposed large company practices and corporate overheads on frustrated former owners accustomed to successfully running their own operations.

My own exposure and experience with the Young Presidents' Organization (YPO) proved very valuable at the time, as did serving on the boards of a half-dozen businesses prior to the years of Apache's diversification. Headquarters passed on plans, controlled capital investment decisions above specific levels, and held quarterly reviews, alternating between onsite and headquarter locations.

When we had acquired enough businesses with similar products in widespread but specialized markets, we grouped the families under group managers within our Apache headquarters. Two of them were Henry Lykken from Honeywell and Richard Christie from General Electric.

Later, as we acquired more unrelated businesses, we turned to Remi Gits, the second generation exponent of a successful family. Unfortunately, Remi was under the spell of his financial and management-consultant–type vice president, Ray Andresen, who from my perspective was nutty and unpragmatic. Although I was not adverse to venturing into waters uncharted by Apache, my assessment of Remi and Ray's projects made me wary.

Three businesses we did not pursue, contrary to Remi's advice that we do so because they were each highly profitable and available at low multiples of earnings, were:

- A West Coast asbestos business whose owners likely had an early perception of the still indiscernible health and environmental risks.

- A gangbusters race track in the south-central United States whose profitability made me wonder if it might not be involved in money laundering and enjoy political and Mafia connections. It certainly seemed to finesse the kind of union labor demands I'd seen bloody the nose of my Yale friend and early partner, Brooks Fields in the racetrack business.

- And finally, a northeastern U.S. maker of many of New York State's highway and freeway road and driver instruction signs. John Kocur visited the sign company facilities with me and we

152

concluded within an hour that their contracts depended on special political arrangements.

In important areas of Apache's diversity, our greatest successes came from internal expansion led both horizontally and vertically by the owner-managers who joined the company. We had three signal successes.

We bought S&J Ranch of Fresno, California (tree crops), in 1970. S&J was led by Rodger Jensen, who had captained a B-29 heavy bomber as a pilot in a number of missions over Tokyo and elsewhere over Japan. Rodger was an outstanding leader, communicator, and manager who grew the business both in terms of acreage of oranges, lemons, olives, figs, and nuts, but also horizontally into processing, packaging, and marketing of high-quality products. He led the industry in the development of quality U.S. pistachios, and Apache into the growth of nursery sales and processing facilities.

Rodger grew our equity from a purchase price of less than $3 million to $90 million when sold to Dole in 1987.

It was the business we least wanted to part with, a comment I passed on to Rodger, age ninety-two, in 2011. Retired Apache director of public affairs David Higgins noted to me, "S&J was the Apache business we made the biggest mistake selling." I quoted David's comment to Rodger, whose response brought tears to my eyes. "Ray, tell David we had and still have something more important going for us, a magnificent sense of mutual respect," a phrase I hope might help others in America, as they pursue their careers.

Les Weisz also did a great, profitable job in expanding Chieftech Auto Parts stores from nineteen stores to over one hundred, entirely through internal, organic growth. When Les and Mildred, his charming wife, decided to retire, fortunately Apache

Rodger Jensen of S&J Ranch.

knew enough to withdraw as well, with $35 million grown from an investment of less than $3 million, in a decade.

In plastic pipe manufacture and sales, we pursued horizontal and vertical expansion. Our original concept was based on the recognition that the manufacture of primarily polyvinyl pipe utilized natural gas, which afforded Apache potential synergies and market potential from capturing more of the spread between well head gas prices and value and service added plastic pipe sales, largely on the West Coast.

Plastic pipe is light but bulky. Pipe is used in agriculture for irrigation worldwide, in constructing water lines in expanding residential areas, and in building and housing. Given the large size of the markets, and the cost of transportation, we set about the strategic acquisition of facilities in separate geographic areas close to primary markets.

We were, however, initially unable, while pursuing our national

Chieftech Auto Parts head Les Weisz sent this picture to me as a joke: "Dear Ray. Hard at work. Everything under control."

strategy, to integrate the managements under the leadership of a motivated, experienced, and successful entrepreneur. Nor were we possessed of sufficient natural gas supply in the right locations to service the pipe plants from our own wells, or to do more than sell our commodity to Dow Chemical, headquartered in Midland, Michigan, or Goodrich, who were giants in this field.

So we changed our strategy, continuing with Harold Wake, former owner and president of Perma Rain. That company's proprietary products were used in the rapidly growing market of drip irrigation, a process in wide usage in Israel and thriftier with water than traditional flood irrigation. Irv Schrum, a superb operator and religious, modest man of high integrity who headed our Stockton, California, pipe business, retained operations of his facilities and took over the balance of our West

With Bill Goettl, head of Goettl Brothers.

Coast operations. The rest of our pipe division businesses we sold, and when Irv informed me he wanted to retire, we asked him to remain on until he had helped us with the sale of his and the balance of our plastic pipe operations. He did and thus added to capital growth and critical mass.

With the spread of conflict in the Near East, the rise of the OPEC cartel, and the takeover by exporting nations of the oil resource base, it became apparent that the timing was propitious for Apache's withdrawal from our widely diversified businesses and return our focus to oil and gas. We understood the underpinnings for long-term increasing oil prices.

Diversification had served us well, and our equity had grown despite having to climb out of our septic tank—like real estate business, while zigging and zagging to survive and grow.

HOLDING THE LINE

AS OUR FUTURE BEGAN TO beckon to our long-chosen primary field of endeavor, the stars lined up for Apache with the significant discovery of the Wyoming Recluse Field. The substance and reality of this discovery enabled us to capitalize not only on the important find, but also with renewed vitality of program sales and organization.

There are few "perfect storms," however, and the seeds of internal dissent had been rumbling for several years. A number of our capable oil people had despaired of our future in oil and gas during the era of far-flung fallen commodity prices and our diversification response. They saw diversity detracting from their chosen field along with the time and efforts of headquarters senior management. Ted Bartling left to go into business for himself, as did several of our senior leaders and geologic personnel, including John Woncik.

At a relatively young age, since my early forties, I had been concerned with having an appropriate successor growing and in residence to succeed me. While John Kocur was a person of great ability, intelligence, and loyalty to me and Apache's long-

157

term goals, which we shared, he and the board recognized that Apache's next leadership generation should have a strong background in oil and gas, which John did not possess. My own was "home grown," lacking both geologic and petroleum engineering training and direct operations experience. Fortunately, John Kocur and I brought other attributes, including perspective and judgment nurtured by analysis of mistakes, to the table.

Jaye Dyer possessed the background, intelligence, and personality to become Apache's future CEO. Those talents were also valuable when applied to our diversified businesses. Jaye was a good sport about being drawn away from oil and gas, which was in a cyclical trough, to meet Apache's far flung needs. He grew rapidly and extensively, but wanted to remain closer to his professional expertise in oil and gas.

While Remi Gits was actively involved beyond running Gits Manufacturing, sugar plums danced before his eyes. He was among several exponents, unfortunately for Apache, who at various points in time advocated splitting the industrial side from the parent company (under Remi's direction, naturally) and turning our oil business over to Jaye.

So for the second time, Remi campaigned for his plan at the board level, but he did not prevail. The "loyalist" group strongly agreed with me and the board that were the business bisected, our relatively small public company would be made smaller and forfeit its hard-fought-for equity and capacity to grow. If ripped apart, Apache's corporate group could not be preserved, nor could its competence in our preeminent program business. We had plans we looked forward to implementing when U.S. oil and gas began to emerge from its cyclical nadir.

With respect to what he termed "the fall from grace of Remi

Jaye Dyer.

Gits," our chairman, Charles Sweatt, had called me from Florida with the curt observation, "You've got another palace revolution on your hands," and went on to explain the split Remi had flown to Palm Beach to propose.

Ray Andresen, Remi's staff consultant whose competence we had been unable to detect, was coming to Minneapolis in days to review numbers and the split concept with our corporate finance group. When he finished up in the late morning, I met him in front of the elevator and noted, "And, oh, by the way, Ray, you're fired." Perhaps his astonishment required a few minutes before he could regroup his thoughts and call Remi.

Since he had traveled to Minneapolis on a Sunday night, Remi was unaware that Apache's treasurer, Carl Hanson, had driven a van to Chicago and entered the Gits' offices that same Sunday night, removing all books and records. Driving through the night, he returned to home base and unloaded, even as Carl

Charles Sweatt and Remi Gits.

joined Andresen and me at the elevator.

I had two more important calls to make, the first to Apache director H. Y. "Ding" Engeldinger, who had been the intermediary in bringing Remi's manufacturing business into Apache. It was important that I close the loop with Ding on that subject clearly and promptly. Ding quickly assessed the situation; although disappointed to accept the outcome, Ding did not jump out of the Apache boat, though obviously the relationship changed.

The next call was to Remi Gits, whom I advised, "We have reached a parting of the ways. You're fired." Remi's response was classic, he not letting on whether his office or Ray Andresen had forewarned him. "I didn't think you had the guts to move. Congratulations."

At my request, Jaye came by my home that evening and executed his letter of resignation. He did, however, repeat his concerns that, although he'd taken on additional corporate responsibilities, his interest and preferred career path lay with the oil business, and while he would do nothing to hurt Apache, he wanted to devote his time and talents to oil and gas. I understood and wished him well, believing his personality, abilities, and motivation would serve his future and his family well. He expressed a desire to remain on Apache's board. I commented that the perception and reality of a conflict of interest was inevitable. Jaye understood, and we parted on good terms—but the interpersonal vessel that had held our own relationship sailed out of our respective lives as we headed down competitive channels after eight important years.

And so we fired Remi Gits and his handmaiden, Ray Andresen, and Jaye became free to go about building a small program oil and gas independent, in which he had a major position, the later sale of which met his aspirations. Regrettably, there also went my first choice of a successor.

ADVENTURE in TELEPHONY

AS PART OF ITS DIVERSIFICATION to counter the cyclical downturn in the oil and gas business, Apache sought out a variety of opportunities. Bob Henretta had brought to my attention an able and competent telephone company man with a strong financial background: Harold Ericson, third-generation owner of the Hector Telephone Company. Harold's stewardship was complemented by the young and efficient Curt Sampson.

Family-owned small telephone companies like Harold's were then in vogue for consolidation as a means of coping with rapid technological change that required massive capital requirements for upgrades. Our plan was to enter the independent telephone industry and then grow through acquisition, using debt leverage and shares of public companies we controlled.

Although we began our partnership with Harold Ericson with external private equity funding, the first two acquisitions chewed up our funding. It became readily apparent and timely that the telephone company had to obtain marketable securities and strong bank credit to continue the growth strategy. This was particularly obvious because several large independents (notably Continental Telephone and United Telephone Company) were rapidly collecting the relatively small population of independents whose long-distance service was closely tied to AT&T, the government-sanctioned monopoly long-distance telephone carrier. So we formed North American Communication Company (NAMCO) as a public company.

Why could we compete and acquire? The small privates had very low after-tax cost basis in their local franchises and the capital gains taxes would be very large in relation to the market value, which was largely a function of the number of phones serviced in their systems. Tax free exchange of stock was thus an attractive acquisition vehicle. This "going public" function was part of my role, as was the arrangement of bank credit.

For credit I turned from our then regular lenders to the First National Bank of St. Paul and its president, Clarence Frame, an Apache program customer and friend. First National agreed to provide us with both acquisition capital and loans for updating the outmoded facilities of acquired telcos. We further leveraged our rural expansion with 2% coupon Rural Electric Association loans, necessary in sparsely populated areas.

Jim Bauman, who had grown up in rural Minnesota, intuitively knew how rural phone companies functioned. He understood the economics and the basis for rapid assimilation of the more sparsely populated telephone franchises, where long-term profitability depended on population growth and higher telephone density. This in turn required service equal to that enjoyed by customers in urban areas, without party lines and human operators. He further understood entrepreneurism, having grown up in the presence of an able, hard-driving father. Jim had majored in business at the University of Minnesota and was to spend his entire illustrious and rewarding career with Apache.

With our publicly owned structure enabling funding, Ericson

Jim Bauman.

and Bauman were able to grow Apache. In our expansion spree, our new brethren, while making fewer smaller company acquisitions, were growing their customer base at a far more rapid rate.

Harold Ericson and I had become good friends. We both owned and flew our private aircraft, and fished in Canada, the Bahamas, and Mexico—a sport we shared enthusiastically.

Harold preferred acquisitions to operations, and so specialized in this field to take advantage of in-depth skills that were Apache's hallmark. Acquisitions of companies in markets shrinking rapidly through consolidation have a characteristic common to climbing an airplane in my own era of piloting, during which pilots passed out as we all did in flight-training simulators. The acquisition analogy to our telephone company development lay in the reality that as values assigned to each telephone served climbed, the thinner the operation's margins and profits—comparable to the lack of oxygen at higher altitudes.

That said, most of my compadres, like myself, had great good fun competing against the odds, sometimes when our little plane's tanks were running on close to empty, whether in World War II, or through the 1980s and mid-'90s, when our strategic drive was critical mass, versus "consistent growth"—the word consistent being antithetical to "how the world works."

The consolidation of the telephone franchises continued, and by 1966 Apache's telephone holdings had grown to 12 telephone companies operating as North American Communication. For Apache to maximize our shareholder return we needed to sell out to one of the larger aggregating independent systems (independent of AT&T), while the competitive market was nearing its peak, but not overstaying the market. We made a very profitable, but more important, timely withdrawal from telephones and significantly added to the adequacy of our equity base, which I popularized with the term critical mass.

Unlike the telephone business, or other utility businesses where franchises are politically limited, the oil and gas basins that source the world's energy business and comprise the world's largest industry are orders of magnitude larger. Rather than a static series of apportioned franchises, they are constantly replenished via technological advances. It was this realization that governed Apache's telephone growth—and that drove the timing of our withdrawal from telecom. (It also ultimately drove our move to expand Apache's oil and gas horizon beyond North America.)

Apache's board at the time did not consider the idea of selling to be as credible as it was to me and our then lead banker, Clarence Frame, president of the First National Bank of St. Paul. I wanted the equity growth within Apache Corp. from a profitable sale. It would provide the critical mass so important to developing Apache Corp. into an outstanding, profitable oil exploration and production company in the world's largest industry—an industry in which there would continue to be running room for up to a century to come.

I sought to avoid disharmony within our small company and at our board level. It became readily apparent to me that I would personally need to develop a strong offer from a suitor for the company that would satisfy employer and shareowners, something Apache's board could not refuse. So I selected an aggressive aggregator whose chairman I knew. He in turn introduced me to Continental Telephone's CEO, Phil Lucier, based in St. Louis.

Phil and I agreed on price and terms.

Unfortunately, Phil was blown up in a St. Louis restaurant parking lot when he turned his ignition key after lunch. (The cause and perpetrators were never determined, and the car bomb appears to have targeted the wrong man.) Continental's chairman, with whom I had dined occasionally in New York City, took over as interim CEO.

The sale of NAMCO to Continental was concluded at year-end 1969. In addition to selling NAMCO for shares of Continental stock, we also wanted and needed to optimize and monetize our then considerable profit. To do so, we sold a portion of our Continental holdings under arrangements agreed to in advance.

We employed a further unique and home-grown strategy, and if we were not the only company to do so, we were the last, for the IRS closed the door after it worked so effectively for

Apache. Apache bought a public offering of debentures convertible into Continental shares of stock and which served as collateral for the consequently cheap financing. What Darrell Egertson, our brilliant controller by title and tax expert in reality, was able to contribute was that when our debt holders converted their Apache debt to Continental shares, which they would do to capture the arbitrage, due to the appreciation of Continental shares above the price when the issue was floated, Apache's loss of Continental stock appreciation was then considered and treated as a tax-deductible capital loss, which offset the capital gains of the Continental shares we held in the Treasury. This loss of the premium we could and did apply against the capital gain realized.

In addition, Apache enjoyed the dividend income from our Continental shares at a taxable rate of 15 percent, versus being fully taxed to the company. As Continental's dividends increased each year, the debenture holders converted to common shares the equity Apache held in the Treasury to accommodate the conversions.

Through these combined means, our NAMCO win was without appreciable tax dilution. Since Clarence Frame's First National Bank of St. Paul had supplied the credit used for the cash portion, we had very low cost basis in our shareholdings either of NAMCO and its successor, in the form of shares resulting from the Continental tax-free exchange.

As we exited the telephone industry and business, our gain in equity and credit capacity was both meaningful and refreshing to our lenders and shareowners as well. I hope we were not smug, but I do know we were delighted, and I hope the reader understands that we had found an entire pony rather than just a needle in the haystack.

APEXCO'S RUN FOR THE ROSES

JAYE DYER'S DEPARTURE FROM APACHE and establishment of his own oil and gas program business created a direct competitor to Apache. Joining Jaye from Apache were Ron Wade, a very able numbers man, and Len Williams on the engineering and production side, who also had an excellent nose for quality oil and gas plays. On the sales side, lacking a sales force beyond himself and his own group of loyalists, Jaye had Hal Olsen, a fine person, and Jim Peterson, whom Whee Whitney had earlier made president of Dain Kalman, one of the largest local brokerage and investment firms. Peterson was also able to reach out to other regional broker dealers and attract customers as the oil price cycle began to turn upward.

In addition to the loyalty of our sales force, we had two factors in our favor: the Recluse oil discovery in Wyoming and the outlook for improving oil prices driven by the OPEC cartel. Our sales force was well aware of the improving investor climate; they were loyal to Apache and largely impervious to other investment opportunities. They also had an advantage they chose to maintain: their customer loyalties, including safeguarding the identity of their Apache customers. These core strengths continued to serve us well, together with credibility and performance.

John Kocur and I also responded by focusing the industrial side of Apache. Internally, I modulated the classic accounting inventory terminologies of inventory evaluation known as "last in, first out," and "first in, first out," we termed the strategy "worst in, first out," being careful to keep the categorization to ourselves at the corporate level, rather than allowing those business units marked for disposition to cease laying their fine eggs. After all, our non-oil and gas divisions employed five thousand people who were providing the bulk of Apache profitability, and John Kocur and I did not want to alienate them. Indeed, our best industrial operators still needed to grow and continue to profit as we shifted our emphasis back to a growth strategy in our program oil and gas business.

Apache accomplished the requisite corporate tuning with the able assistance of Charlie Hahn, Henry See, and Phil Byers, the latter from the operations side of our business. This enabled John Black, in charge of exploration under Byers's direction, to make the transition, as the cliché goes, "seamlessly."

Kocur and I also evolved a new corporate structure, the better to align our program investors with our oil and gas operations. A separate publicly held entity, owned by program investors and Apache Corp., would align those interests. We conceived that investors could, if they so chose, exchange their program units for shares in the entity with the gains tax either deferred until sold or fully eliminated through charitable donations. The resultant public company was dubbed Apache Exploration Company—Apexco.

From Apache's perspective, for purposes of retaining control and for funding large-scale operations requirements within a discrete oil and gas entity equipped for larger business transactions, it was important to exchange our oil assets for shares to meet very specific IRS requirements. The result provided a growth of earnings, cash flows, reserves, and production—in other words, critical mass.

Dealing with employee restlessness meant moving some of our key operations people. We offered some of them stock options in the new company. The single most important hurdle was among several people with strong personal loyalties to Apache and to me personally. Their concern was that this step might represent moving away from the Apache corporate umbrella. Yet they accepted the change, led by John Black, our exceptionally able oil and gas-finding geologist, and George McLernon, our able and experienced vice president of operations; Phil Byers and Charlie Hahn handled the headquarters linkage very well.

Kocur and I also realized we should bring to the new oil and gas entity a chief executive officer and several high-profile, seasoned, and respected former oil executives to serve on its board. Fenelon Boesche, respecting the timing and direction, agreed to serve on the board of the Apache Exploration Company and participated both in the selection of the new CEO, Ken Reed (the former president of Amerada Hess), and the election of John Hamilton, who had been Reed's boss at Amerada Hess, to the board. They were joined on the board by a former senior executive of Hudson Bay Oil & Gas, a subsidiary then of Union Oil of California, and his counterpart who had worked with the legendary Paul Getty, the oilman and former Minnesotan. (Getty had built his worldwide oil powerhouse through exploration and a series of acquisitions that included Skelly, Tidewater, and

Henry See.

Warren Petroleum.) From the Apache side, I joined as chairman of the board of Apexco, along with Howard Alkire, Apache director and chairman of the executive committee; Mike Belzer, Apache director; Malcolm Mackay; and Bob Collins, our then Apache vice president of finance.

Apache's program sales force was allotted a small spiff for explaining the new entity to our program investors, many of whom welcomed the added liquidity of their oil and gas investments. The combination's advantages, which included timing, were elegant, and the response exceptional. The new company got under way strongly capitalized because Apache did not transfer its oil division debt, receiving instead a greater number of shares. It was very important that we provided alternatives to the tax-free exchange for shares; they could continue to retain their interests in their then form, or they could accept shares in

Charles Hann.

another Apache formed company where the exchange would be taxable. That entity, Key Production Company, would not seek new reserves, but rather produce and pay out liquidating dividends taken largely as a return of capital.

Apache unit holders who exchanged received one share of stock for each $10.00 of independent engineers' appraisal value of reserves, (attested by a fairness opinion from an investment banking firm and thorough review by Arthur Andersen). The shares paid a modest cash dividend that the shareholders appreciated. Investors also liked the debt-free nature of Apexco. And Apache welcomed the Apexco dividend since it was the sole means of obtaining a cash yield on our equity. Seven years later, we grew by another $70 million.

With gas and oil prices rising, our exploration and production team more than pulled its share of the wagon, making a series of gas and condensate discoveries in the deep Anadarko Basin of Oklahoma, led by the Springer Sand development at

(In back, left to right) Howard Alkire, President of Apexco, Ken Reed, Mike Belzer, and Harvey Engeldinger, and (seated) yours truly and Charles Sweatt in 1972.

a prospect called Chickasha that, in 1973-74, dwarfed our previously compelling Recluse Field in Wyoming, discovered in 1967. Chalk up another great find for John Black, who not only made the decisions but had acquired significant acreage ahead of the play. Virtually all of the acreage proved productive and we had a bonanza.

Our program investors enjoyed outstanding performance, and Apexco shares spurted, as did Apexco stock and cash dividends; the stock dividends brought the cost down from $10.00 a share to $7.00. By the time we sold the company to Natomas seven years after starting it, the $7.00 per share had appreciated 450 percent to $31.50. Hmmm . . . as Apache owned over 50 percent of Apexco, acquired both in the exchanges and subsequent purchases, its rapid growth was helping with our overall transition from a mini-conglomerate toward our long-range target of becoming an independent oil and gas company—a target set back in 1954.

THE APEXCO ENDGAME

HOWEVER, THE APEXCO CHAPTER WAS but half complete—
for internally within Apexco our CEO Ken Reed dreamed of
a larger, more autonomous role for himself, and for a fortune
commensurate with his desire for complete independence. Ken
tested these waters with Kocur and me, quietly extolling the
presumed virtues of gradual separation leading to full independence. He illuminated the then familiar game plan previously
fancied and embraced by Truman Anderson and then Remi
Gits. "Here we go again," Kocur and I concurred privately.

Ken was a first-class host to his board from Tulsa and the Minneapolis members and Apache representatives alike, the latter
being substantial investors in our drilling programs. To a person
they enjoyed the Tulsa reception dinners the night before board
meetings. Ken's tales of success from the gas fields earned him
a strong following among the board, though he was rapidly losing any basis of support from among the operations people.

The first of the former Apache senior oil people against

whom Ken moved was the very bright, capable, and loyal George McLernon. I blame myself for being slow and blind-sided and failing to head off the firing of George—Ken obtained permission to do so at a board meeting, in a surprise move. George had made outstanding contributions to Apache over the years; even as Ken turned against him, George was capturing the gas stream at a Recluse gas processing plant that he had assembled from parts he found around the country and pieced together efficiently. This had enhanced our profitability to such a degree that Apexco ran afoul of the excess profits tax and we found ourselves being penalized rather than allowed the rewards of the marketplace for exceptional savings of otherwise wasted hydrocarbons and products. We were, for example, stripping out propane and butane and making money processing products we had sold for as little as 3¢ per gallon (compared with forty and fifty times greater in value a few years later).

George inspired the loyalty of his employees and also made good on the development of natural gas production from large, old, but highly productive West Texas shallow gas fields. After he was fired by Ken, George obtained funding support from Apache director Curt Carlson. Because of the conflict of interest, Curt resigned from Apache's board of directors—a loss to the board. Fortunately he also remained loyal to Apache's programs, and to Apexco, Apache, and me. George also had significant and highly profitable holdings in Apache. George and Curt did very well in their venture and George's hustle and ability rewarded him with a significant uplift to his financial well-being and self-esteem. George and I remained good friends until his death from cancer.

Ken's next move was against John Black, again in an end run. This time, there were no dice, but blood was let. The basis for Ken's charges against Black was both astounding and crude.

Apache directors and officers convene on Curt Carlson's boat in the mid-1960s. Seated from left to right: Bardon Higgins, George McLernon, Curt Carlson, Charles Sweatt, Raymond Plank, H.Y. Engeldinger, A.E. Barton, Malcolm Mackay. Officers standing, left to right: James DeVille, John Black, Jaye Dyer, M.S. Belzer (a director), Henry G. Lykken, and Charles Hann.

One of the geologists who had reported to John left Apexco to go out on his own. The Chickasha field found by John Black, long in the making, was a relatively shallow major gas play over a long trend of acreage known as a stratigraphic trap. Apache had acquired very substantial acreage along the trend. The play concept and acreage acquisition had actually begun several years earlier, with the discovery of the adjacent, shallow Marchand oil sand paralleling the gas and condensate play.

At a board dinner the evening before the next day's meeting, Ken charged John with having been careless in the protection of proprietary information concerning Chickasha. There was nothing proprietary about it; the magnitude of the discovery was obvious not only to me, but to the industry as well. The only relevant question was how far the play might extend. The field continued to expand to the northwest. Apache's former geologist had acquired a small position after leaving Apache.

John Black had argued to the geologist that the ethical thing for him to do would be to turn over his acreage to Apache. John was persuasive even as he was under direct attack from Reed. I drew the line with the Apexco directors and at the relevant Apache board meeting, reminding the Apache board that while representing Apexco, they bore responsibilities to Apache's program investors and Apache as well. And I damned well didn't want Apexco and Apache to lose both McLernon *and* Black to Reed's game plan.

With our VP of finance, Bob Collins, who was an Apexco director but not an Apache director, I made my position unequivocally clear, and in doing so made a near fatal error. Collins embraced the Reed approach and as an Apexco director perhaps thought significant discoveries grew on trees. I told Collins that Apache and Apexco could not, in my opinion, survive the loss of both George and John, and if Bob persisted in supporting Ken's arrogant contriving and isolation from his people, I'd take Apexco apart "brick by brick and throw them at him."

Bob's response was to send a letter within a day to the Apache board in which he formally charged me with working against the interests of the Apexco shareholders, calling on the board for appropriate action.

The Apache board, recognizing its responsibilities, requested an independent investigation. To do this, they turned to a respected, retired federal judge in Illinois, who after several months found for me over Collins. Because Collins had previously told both Kocur and me that he was getting close to retiring, we assumed that his protest had been fostered for the purpose of a more generous than standard retirement package. The board advised me they would handle his severance; I did not choose to find out the amount.

That left John and me with the underlying issue of Mr. Reed's desires to separate Apexco and Apache. We concluded it was time for the Apexco shareowners to take a gain exceeding $100 million off the table, by developing an appropriate offer for Apexco that the shareholders would joyfully accept, and that the Apache directors also could not refuse. In September 1977, Apache sold Apexco to the Natomas Company of San Francisco for $127 million.

Our people plan involved integrating the Apexco operating staff back into Apache, as well as negotiating with the purchaser an arrangement whereby they would continue to service our drilling program market until our internally generated projects and competent staff could replenish inventory.

Our people were thrilled. They were relieved of Ken Reed, a boss they deplored. (They liked and respected Phil Byers, the company's senior exploration officer.) They had money in their bank accounts from their Apexco shares and options that had multiplied handsomely. Apache enjoyed a high oil funding ability from the Apexco sale, and with its significant capital resources quickly replenished acreage. In contrast, Natomas floundered.

Reed landed at Natomas as a senior oil executive—until Natomas went down to a hostile takeover and Apache got its properties back. (What goes around comes around!) I had read of that pending takeover of Natomas in the *Wall Street Journal* and on the day of the announcement contacted the CEO of the takeover company. I had a pretty good idea as to what specific Natomas assets, largely in Indonesia from a non-Apache origin, they would seek to retain. The telephone conversation went something like this: "You probably have found in your due diligence process that Apache has a lawsuit against Natomas that we intend to pursue for breach of contract and expect to win. Having no fault to find with you, we'd like to repurchase from you the properties that we sold to Natomas, and would be pleased to drop the litigation." We agreed to meet following the closing of the Natomas purchase and were able to close a transaction that enabled us to recover the assets we had sold in the first place, less our Canadian remnants and our interest in the North Sea Buchan Field.

So, we got our people and our properties back, plus some of the properties that Natomas had developed in the interim. We found Natomas had been curtailing the sale of gas from our old favorite, the Chickasha Field. A different buyer, intrastate versus interstate, bought at a somewhat lower price for substantially higher volumes of gas, which we delivered. We recovered the $160 million repurchase price we paid in less than three years.

Many of the Apexco assets continued to produce years later. In July 2011, I conversed with a successor to John Black in Apache's Central Region. Having learned that Apache finders in the deep Anadarko Basin were doing very well in their current drilling, I asked highly able Rob Johnston, our regional VP, where they were having the greatest success this year. His response was instant, "Acreage Apache acquired between 1970 and 1977, where current technology and drilling are again yielding great results." Acreage acquired by John Black, who had established truly outstanding investor programs between 1970 and 1974, which added several hundred million dollars for program customers and shareholders alike.

THE UNIVERSITY
OF MINNESOTA

AS THERE IS AN IMPORTANT distinction between accomplishing a long-term and a short-term objective, I want to comment on that which, to me, is as important as an objective accomplished: "What has one learned?" From this springs the secret seven-league boots of happiness, fulfillment, and successively larger challenges, and the open secret of the importance of lifetime learning across a universe of opportunities for those who understand and elect to match challenge with personal commitment.

Would it be too obvious to note that learning moves up the fulfillment scale in direct proportion to its transference by achieving? Apache's corporate journey, though measured in twenty-three years by 1979, had "only just begun." A number of our investors fared better; applying portions of their large percentage win to their favorite charitable interest to which we now turn.

We had formed Apache from a concept and with a plan. By 1969, well before Apexco and the upsurge of the cyclical oil business, we'd reached the initial benchmark I'd set. If we were

Apache Corp. lists on the NYSE on May 27, 1969 under the symbol APA. From left: Charles Hann, Jaye Dyer, Carl Hanson, me, Philip West, and Henry Lykken.

to be a successful, profitable company built to last, then a primary goal was to be listed on the New York Stock Exchange. We felt good about our listing in 1969, and had by then set other long-term objectives.

When we sold Apexco, of the cash realization of $127 million, Apache's largest sale transaction to that time, the public shareholders realized $53 million. Apache, which had been acquiring stock in the open market, realized $74 million, out of which Uncle Sam and the states of Oklahoma and Minnesota took the sizeable cash tax bite of $20 million.

Two Minneapolis families, headed by Curtis Carlson and John Cowles, respectively, availed themselves of the appreciation of Apexco shares to the substantial benefit of the University of Minnesota.

Kenneth Hacking, President of the NYSE, yours truly, and Jimmie Nick, the floor specialist in our stock.

Curt was credited with having built Minnesota's largest fortune through a combination of businesses originally based on Gold Bond stamps, which merchants gave out for almost everything from groceries and drugs to services, major appliances, and automobiles during the heyday of stamps as promotional tools. Curt began his entrepreneurial career delivering newspapers, later attending the University of Minnesota. He was an avid learner and builder who valued opportunities associated with tax incentives. These were inherent in promotional stamps, until they became so common nationally that retailers as a group turned away from them.

The tax advantage lay in the fact that there was very little history from which to determine what percentage of the stamps purchased by a retail clientele would be redeemed for merchandise. Therefore, the stamp companies were able to defer taxes on a significant percentage of the revenues collected while utilizing growing reserves for taxes to parlay into other forms of endeavor. Stamp businesses could largely defer taxes until the stamps were redeemed for merchandise. These reserves could be reinvested in other businesses or set aside in financial instruments, kindred on both fronts to the underlying principles applied by insurance companies—life or casualty, and as applied, of course, by Warren Buffett.

Curt was astute both to the point of recognizing that stamps were not forever and that he needed to redeploy the cash gold mine into other forms of tax-incentivized businesses—hotels, for example. His next major outreach commenced with the venerable but strategically centered Radisson hotels, which he extended to most major cities across the United States and beyond to the Bahamas, the Soviet Union, Japan, and Spain, where he was approached by the dictator, General Franco.

Needless to say, he recognized the tax incentives inherent during that era of our oil investor program business in which he built up a large repertoire of unit holdings suitable for tax incentives. He acquired a large position in Apache, of which he held, he told me, every share into his eighties. He must have captured a large portion of the over 3,675-fold increase from 4 cents per share.

The John Cowles Sr. family was another in our loyal Minnesota customer base, having gradually increased annual program participation and share holdings over a number of years. The Cowles family fortune had derived from John and his brother Gardner's media empire. It included, at one point, *Look* magazine, the *New Republic*, and *Harper's*, plus radio and television stations and a wide array of newspapers. Under John's direct ownership were Minneapolis's two major newspapers, the dominant radio and television network stations WCCO, and other television stations and newspapers including that in Buffalo, New York, later sold to become part of Warren Buffett's empire.

Before John Sr. became a serious Apache investor, through his internal tax manager, Dave Brown, he kindly invited me to his business fishing and hunting retreat. The shooting was marvelous, their raised ducks and geese augmented by flocks of wild birds attracted during migration to their bird lake and surrounding grain fields. After-dinner discussion invariably involved a prominent leader from academia, president, or foreign affairs mogul. I cherished the many outings I had there. John Sr. and I were also bridge partners—a game we both enjoyed, but one which, though we played for but small stakes, John was as pleased to lose as I was to win. I think John may have reveled at my pain when he would call out "seven spades" or "six no trump," which he played very well, particularly without the cards to accompany the call. However, I gained John's trust, and with it his respect and substantial annual investments, which Dave Brown and even Dave's charming wife, Florence, watched over with the eyes of eagles.

Curt—then the Chairman of the University of Minnesota Foundation—"had plans for me" and announced to the board and me simultaneously my new role in developing deferred giving. This assignment, from Apache's largest individual shareholder and drilling program investor, was something I couldn't refuse.

The first initiative I took was to select and persuade a group of University of Minnesota dedicated alums to form our "Brainstorm Committee" and initially to meet for luncheon frequently at a room within the IDS Tower of downtown Minneapolis.

One luncheon, held between the announcement of the Apexco sale and its consummation, had particularly beneficial ramifications.

When I returned to my office from the luncheon, held at the Alumni Club in the IDS Tower, my first call was to Curt, to whom I addressed the following:

"Curt, have I got a deal for you. Julie Davis [a prominent Minneapolis lawyer actively involved with the foundation] has got you tabbed with a ten-million-dollar tag for the University of Minnesota. But it's bargain day. You can give me five, and here's how you pay for it. You have about a thirty cents per share tax cost basis in your Apexco shares, which are now selling above thirty dollars. They'll cover the gift, and you'll end up paying no gains tax by deducting the five million."

Curt laughed and said, "Sold. Follow up, would you, with Chet"—his tax guru.

"Thanks, Curt; will do."

Elapsed time? About two minutes.

I then called John Cowles' tax handler Dave Brown on his private line, and the conversation went like this:

"Dave, I'm aware that John Cowles's favorite university is Harvard, and he's paying off a gargantuan pledge. But here's the idea. Your newspapers, radio, and TV stations in Minnesota drive John's fortune, and the university is conspicuously absent from his significant philanthropy. Yet your writers for your liberal rag and a number of your announcers are University of Minnesota products. You've got a pile of virtually no-cost-basis Apexco shares we've contracted to sell with Apexco to Natomas. With several million dollars, there could be a Cowles School of Journalism at the University of Minnesota."

And so there were the two related gifts reaching around $7 million.

At the same brainstorm session we came up with the concept and plan for the Hubert Humphrey Institute. We dispatched John Whaley, our star foundation closer, to Washington to meet with the senator.

Our brainstorming group, which included a great friend and fellow university devotee, Don Padilla, had informed us at lunch of news not yet public: that Hubert was dying from cancer. We each knew and respected Hubert and understood the importance of the timing in contacting him for the purpose intended. John Whaley called me from Washington following his productive meeting with Hubert concerning the Cowles School. He reported Hubert's comments: "I like the concept very much, but don't you think the Hubert Humphrey Institute has a little better ring to it?"

Of course, we did, and in Hubert's name we were to raise $13 million in a matter of months, most of it coming from beyond Minnesota, including as I recall, around $3 million from admirers from Great Britain and Japan.

It had been quite a lunch and brainstorming session among creative people meeting on a selfless cause, on a participation basis, comprising marvelous tools coupled with goals well beyond self-interest—the kinds of goals that still distinguish caring Americans from the greedy.

APACHE'S JOHN BLACK ERA

JOHN BLACK WAS ATTENDING THE University of Tulsa, where he was majoring in geology, when he joined Apache as a summer geology department intern. In addition to mapping prospects as part of his daily dozen, John was encouraged by John Woncik and other senior Apache geologists to practice what he was learning, by developing leads and possible prospects suitable for exploration. During his initial summer in our Tulsa office he came up with two prospects that he believed had trapped commercial hydrocarbons. The background and important, highly effective teaching of John Woncik commanded the respect for Black's first leads, which he had confirmed as worthy of exploration by reviewing the drilling logs of other wells in the areas of his focus. (Analysis always included study of the area's wells where hydrocarbon shows had been recorded.) His mentors liked the work and the prospecting, and John's first two wells drilled became commercial discoveries for an Apache drilling program.

Formally joining Apache directly from college, John Black, like John Woncik, thought in three dimensions. His first two

John Black at an Apache site in the Anadarko Basin.

discoveries proved not to be accidental. John went on to become a significant and highly respected gas and oil finder, largely in Oklahoma. When Jaye Dyer and Apache parted company with John Woncik, who left earlier to go on his own, John Black and his right hand, Phil Livingston, took charge of our oil finding function. John Black's successful tenure with Apache overlapped the procedures of essentially starting over in the oil business, but not the program business, twice during our first fifty years.

Along with tracking our year-end reserves, and utilizing the formal measurements then required by the SEC, at the end of each year Apache tracked the future gross income at then prevailing commodity prices. "Gross income" was essentially oil and gas future revenues before being reduced by operating costs, regional and corporate overhead, transportation costs, plugging liabilities, interest costs, severance, and income taxes. It was only one of a number of benchmarks. Its significance, however, was the meagerness of "future gross income" after Apache's interests were exchanged into Apexco for shares of stock. That number was a minute $35 million.

By the time we sold Apexco to Natomas, our internal measurements had changed to match regulatory nomenclature, as gross "income" no longer possessed relevance. We then measured in barrels of oil, equating gas to oil to arrive at a single number, on the basis of the hydrocarbon energy ratio of 6,000 cubic feet of gas to one barrel of oil. Our year-end 1977 reserve report showed 7.8 million barrels of oil, which at $6 per barrel of oil (and $1 per mcf of gas) might have approximated $60 million. Not much to show for the seven years of Apexco, for the simple reason that the oil reserves did not give credit to the $74 million pretax gain from the sale of Apexco, which became part of our base for what was essentially our third entrée into the oil business.

By 1977 we faced another battle beyond the risks associated with finding oil and gas. Following our successful offering to the public of a $10 million drilling program, we were confronted by a thorough, in-depth Securities and Exchange investigation that shut off our program market for nearly a year before we were allowed to resume program sales. At the time, the delay was totally frustrating; and its frustrations were not limited to the swarms of agents and their requests for masses of data. Despite the zeal of their search we were cleared without sanction or penalty. Hardships and apprehension were associated with the painful exercise, however.

Only years later did we discern either the reason for the complaint or its source. We came to understand that the complaint had perhaps been launched by Paine Webber Jackson and Curtis, with whom we had an agreement that they would limit their oil program sales to Apache's programs. When Paine Webber found renewed and growing interest in drilling programs, we studied a number of the programs they sponsored, some of which we felt were inappropriate for public consumption and the sale of which would detract from Apache-originated products. Rather than litigate, as they were busily offering the products of others, we cut them off from our own list of broker dealers. In reality, several of their program sponsors may have done more damage to their clients' financial well-being than cigarette smoking does to human lungs.

I remain fond of the observation that those who lack self-respect are unlikely to enjoy the respect of others—or credibility. At the time, little did we know that what appeared to be a potential disaster would turn out to be a blessing, though well disguised from Kocur and me.

The Securities and Exchange Commission had delayed us from presenting our program to prospects while they scrutinized us. Not anticipating delay of our registration statement, Apache had negotiated terms of farm-ins to gain inventory and accepted drilling commitments, and had contracted for drilling rigs during a period of high oilfield service company demand (driven by cyclically rising prices). We chose to honor those contracts rather than seek to negotiate our way out of them and used Apache's capital to do so. During that period as the prospects had to be drilled we made a series of important discoveries while temporarily delayed by the SEC. Of course when we were cleared by the SEC further drilling was done on behalf of our customers. Fortunately the choice was simple. Integrity mandated it.

For Apache's long-term growth the pending disaster became a double bonanza. Between December 31, 1977, and year-end 1978, our reserves increased, admittedly from a small base, to 17.7 million barrels from fields that continued to grow. (This acreage would still produce in 2005, though at lower but still profitable levels.) Formations such as the Granite Wash west of Elk City, Oklahoma, and the Atoka were appropriately commented on by our then superb land man A. J. Mason, who noted the rocks were so porous, it was like "drilling into hamburger."

The successes Apache's John Black, Phil Livingston, and A.J. Mason racked up for Apache's account also spurred our program business. In the areas where successful drilling for our own account opened up, our geologists and land men pounced on additional acreage like hungry cats gobbling mice. Program sales and financial results for investor groups, Apache, and programs soared. John Black had earlier spread gigantic maps on the walls and conference tables that illustrated how fields had been found around the rim of Oklahoma's Deep Anadarko Basin. Those fields marched up to the deeper portions of the basin, to that point then limited by seismic, drilling, and completion technology. John noted, "And here is where the next significant finds will be made."

We entered the Deep Anadarko through our giant spread obtained from Bob Hefner, an Oklahoma operator with extensive acreage in an Apache venture. David Higgins and Roger Plank observed that this qualified Apache as a company willing to embark upon and accept real risk, an assessment represented in the title of our first corporate history, *Journey into Risk Country.*

Here is the inside story. One day in my Minneapolis office, I received one of John Black's calls, with the stirring words, "Ray, I've finally found a way you can be of help to Apache's growth." (A tinge of sarcasm frequently laced our years of close friend dialogue.) "Bobby Hefner is about as full of bullshit as you are, Plank, and I want you to join me in Tulsa. We'll meet him in Elk City and acquire his spread, called the North Block." He made the appointment, and I trundled to the airport, flew to Tulsa in my little bird, and together we kept our 1:30 p.m. appointment. I was to do the talking, and found myself perhaps a bit more nervous, given John's challenge, than if I were the featured luncheon speaker to five hundred or a thousand souls.

After an hour or so, while Bobby Hefner showed some interest, it was apparent we weren't getting anywhere. There had to be a reason. And then it dawned on me. He needed money, badly—money his lenders had learned not to advance beyond limits already reached. So I took a shot at it. "Bob, while we're not flush with cash, we'll carry you for an interest in the wells we'll agree to drill, pay you five million up front, and agree to loan you five million that you can either repay out of oil and gas sales, or pay in advance should you sell off some of the resulting production." Hefner's face lit up. We agreed to terms within minutes and left his office with the North Block, he soon to receive the $10 million, funded by the share sale of Apexco.

Kocur points out that we bet the farm and won the bet—true risk. We sold off an undivided interest in a portion of the northernmost acreage to Jaye Dyer's Dyco, which helped him make it, and began to sprinkle the terrain with gas and condensate discoveries. Bobby had been spared—temporarily. While we had obtained certain rights, Bob soon needed more money, and sold off substantial additional acreage to Mobil. To complete that sale, while it was possible for Hefner to retain operating rights, it became important to him to get rid of our creditor position. So he paid Apache off in full the $5 million loan and was able, for a period, to keep up with the costs of his share of our development wells.

Mobil was not so fortunate. When they had been called on by Hefner's company for drilling costs, Mobil paid, but their funds, rather than being available to the specific drilling, had been spread around and were unavailable when Hefner hit the wall. Mobil requested that Apache join the creditor's committee to recoup costs, an invitation Kocur respectfully declined. We got our money but not as a common creditor, while Mobil unfortunately, I assume, may have had to pay twice. As John Black said to me, "You guys really did okay."

MY POLITICAL EVOLUTION

MY FIRST DISTINCT MEMORY OF a presidential election dates from age ten in November 1932. I was seated with my parents in the dining room after dinner, listening to election news of the race between President Herbert Hoover and Franklin Delano Roosevelt. I remember the radio set, long before television, with its crackling transmission. Father was an ardent Republican; we were a Republican family. As Republicans, we feared "the worst." The United States was in a deep depression, and Americans, blaming Hoover, wanted change. The basis for Republican roots was straightforward: a strong work ethic, strong commitment to individual freedom versus collectivism, and no ambivalence whatsoever that unions were overreaching, even though we occasionally, begrudgingly credited them with having accomplished good things, such as improving underground coal mine safety and providing better compensation for U.S.-based blue-collar jobs.

During my high school years, the study of history and world geography fascinated me, and later Yale and World War II added an international perspective. It would have been impossible not to be interested in the political and governmental aspects of evolving lifetime learning.

Here, too, my father's perspectives, based both on a strong work ethic and the business challenges he shared with me, contributed to my conservative preferences with respect to local and state government. For example, as president and controlling shareholder of his printing firm, Harrison and Smith, a major thorn in my father's side was union opposition to plant modernization, based on unions' resistance to advancing technology to protect jobs. While he was a local Minneapolis employer, local companies as well as larger businesses from Chicago and New York competed heavily in local printing markets. It seemed to my father that the larger businesses were the pacesetters in technology advancement, cost reduction, and lower pricing, leaving them better able to offset transportation costs associated with being farther removed by distance from local markets.

Throughout college it was easy for me to name consecutively the U.S. presidents, their opponents, and most of the vice presidents. I've followed every presidential election over the ensuing decades and hundreds of lesser campaigns, being involved personally and directly with perhaps more than my share.

Another vivid presidential campaign was in 1940, during my first boy and girl house party at the Sheldon's Encampment forest cabin where I first met and liked Sally Stevens. The guests included Yale-bound 1940 Blake graduates, Al Sheldon (the host), Stu Hanson, Phil Duff, Ken Dayton, as well as Al's sister Anne, Sally, probably June Lee Jackson, and maybe Mary "Bug" Kennedy. We were interested in Wendell Willkie, who later earned the nomination of the Republicans to oppose FDR's third term bid. We didn't talk much politics at the Sheldon's, but did on the trip back to Minneapolis while also listening to campaign news on the radio. Later that fall, as a freshman, I was thrilled when Willkie visited Yale and spoke to us on the Green in his strained, husky voice.

Four years later, in B-24 night flight training, I remember picking up the Roosevelt-Dewey campaign as we flew over the Hoover Dam and recall being the only crew member interested. On returning from the war, although I'd come to respect Harry Truman primarily for being a stronger, more decisive president than I'd anticipated, Dewey was favored to win against Truman. As a Republican, I slightly favored Dewey despite my great regard for Truman. Perhaps this period was the source of my earliest doubts over the relative righteousness of the Republicans, who seemed not always to travel the value road I'd associated with clearly differentiated principles in that era.

In Minneapolis politics, Hubert Humphrey ran for mayor in 1943. He and my wife Sally had come to know and regard three active young Democratic-Farmer-Labor (DFL) protégés: Walter Mondale, later ambassador to Japan, senator, and vice president; Orville Freeman, later governor who advanced no farther; and Doug Frazer, who followed a conscientious career in the U.S. House of Representatives and became a good Minneapolis mayor. Earlier I had helped Sally stuff envelopes for Humphrey and felt no heresy. Through Sally I came to know these DFL rising stars and found them bright and rational, albeit on the other side.

However, the Republican Party appealed. I volunteered in the trenches, serving at two or more state election cycles on the Platform Policy Committee, which appealed greatly because ostensibly that's where the principles were to be defined on which our candidates would run. I did not know then how little it was to matter, as platforms based on principles and programs become victims of polls and media. But then it was positions and issues I cared about and fervently pleaded for at local, county, and state conventions.

One of my long-persisting high-minded values was to pick and elect a candidate whose principled views were closely allied to mine, and then let go of him or her to discharge the duties of office as each saw fit. I did not feel it appropriate to press the elected official (unless on the other side and uninformed on an issue such as energy) with my views, particularly where I found a self-conflicted interest. I strongly felt self-interest could and would detract from the office holder's doing his duty, which neither included being reelected nor self-enrichment. The failure of so many to meet my tests of platform and principles rapidly became a source of my disillusionment, which ranged from disappointment to outrage.

As I began to become active in party organization, and before I began actively raising money, I thought for a time that I might pursue both a business and a political career. I ran for and was quietly elected (almost appointed or anointed) to the Wayzata City Council. I ran for mayor, and was defeated. The defeat stemmed in large part from the reserve of my campaign. I'd expected to carry the day based on accomplishment as a council member, and with values I thought should appeal. Sweet naïveté. I probably also misgauged my impact and reach. I trace this back to my high school debate days: When the debate coach preferred I debate on both sides of one year's issue, "Should the government own the railroads?" I insisted on going only with the negative—despite railroads' rapacious ways. I was totally opposed to featherbedding and union control, and insisted federal bureaucracy was not an acceptable alternative.

It was also first during high school debating that I found my delivery style, which was particularly appealing at the emotional level. I found that sprinkling my delivery with analogies carried my positions a long way. Possibly my memory is convenient; I do not recall losing a debate, and I do clearly recall that my style evoked interest and applause that at times befuddled my opponents.

That approach, together with delivering a talk without the benefit of a script, has served me increasingly well over the decades on subjects too numerous to note. As hinted above, however, it began to become clear to me that I had a serious choice to make. Campaigning and serving were not all there was to persuading an audience attuned audiovisually. There could be immense time tradeoffs and drudgery. The best man with the best positions often didn't win. Rather than my becoming a businessman politician, the careers had to be separated. I would pursue business and not political office. For me, it was the right answer.

UNIONS, CIVIC INVOLVEMENT, AND CIVIL RIGHTS

UNIONS, AS THEY BECAME INVOLVED in people-related political issues, began as a positive force in one opposed to the
moral and economic well-being of a major segment of the work
force. As time passed however, the pursuit of union power to
serve their members' interests, led to overreaching abuse of the
public and workers alike as enabled by federal and state legisla-
tion.

My father's small, but quality printing business, along with
the newspapers suffered when technological advances were
blocked by strikes: he lost business to plants in Chicago and
New York whose purchases of state of the art equipment increased productivity.

It was during the 1940s through 1960s that I grew up and
became more critical than supportive of the power wielded by
the federal government as unions themselves were denying the
right to work. Unions themselves miscarried with a remarkable
level of corruption involving large amounts of money diverted
from worthy to objectionable ends. The rights of the union
rank and file were abused, and U.S. products were lost—along

with jobs—to more competitive markets abroad.

One of the reasons why I entered the oil and gas exploration and production business, but did not pursue horizontal integration and refining, was that unionized refining was corrupt. Organized labor created costs beyond our control; in the field of exploration, conversely, we could chart our own course. With the refining and delivery of gasoline the primary destination for petroleum products, vertical integration held undeniable appeal and the allure of a much larger company. But judging by the multiple business failures among the medium-sized refiners who looked to vertically integrate, Apache maintained a better course by avoiding refining and distribution.

Union-related issues dominated a full year in Apache's plastic pipe business, run by Irv Schrum in Stockton, California. Irv wanted to eliminate two positions on each of several production lines, and was struck by his local union.

The tactics of the opposing forces included entering the plant on a Sunday through the roof and cutting the electric power lines within the plant; setting fire to the two-acre pipe storage yard to burn the pipe inventory; decorating the plant and storage trucking areas with sharp metal tire punchers that resulted in multiple flat tires on the eighteen-wheelers; and setting up an observation and assault post a block away from which the angry, largely imported "goons" fired steel balls at our workers' and staff people's cars from power slingshots. Those who crossed the picket lines were noted, traced to their homes, and threatened along with their wives and children.

Irv had, however, been compiling photographic evidence of the "excessive behavior." At a Chamber of Commerce luncheon attended at the request of the mayor and police chief of

Stockton, Irv made a compelling visual and verbal case, noting this important local business was owned by a national company with other nonunion plants. If the strike were not halted, who among the chamber's luncheon attendees would be next, and what would be the city's position if Apache closed the plant and other businesses were hit?

Following this luncheon, the police chief and mayor drove to the plant site, where the angry strikers made a fatal error. A steel ball penetrated a side door of the chief's car, and the plant went on about its competitive business on a non-union basis, voting the union out.

In the same general time frame in Minneapolis, I had succeeded as head of the Young Men of Minnesota an energetic young man named Wayne Field. By the late 1970s, another young man from Minnesota, Larry Wilson, took it upon himself, with my support, to cross a picket line and access the Research Laboratory of General Mills, which one of the company's unions had brought under siege.

P.K. Peterson was the newly elected Republican mayor. I had run his campaign and finance effort. I was interested in observing whether visitors to the facility would be granted access. We had been told by the mayor that the police were onsite to see that access was assured, and that marching pickets were maintaining the required distance between each other without impeding ingress or egress to or from the facility. Larry found access blocked, as did I.

Following Larry's discouraging report, I decided on a personal visit. It proved a classic. I was accosted by an elderly woman wearing pink gloves, who pulled brass knuckles over her gloves and spoke with me in the presence of a very large man carrying a small club. "And where do you think you're going?"

I replied, "Inside."

"Oh, no, you're not," she said, as the very large man drew menacingly closer.

Discretion being the better part of valor, I made my way to the parked police car and learned that the man inside was the police chief, to whom I quoted the mayor's assurances. His rejoinder was that these pickets were largely imported scabs who were angry and would in his opinion precipitate a riot, and people would be injured if not killed. He assured me that because he was being watched, he was not going to escort me into the facility, did not want a riot and that I would do well to leave the area before becoming the initial casualty. I followed his advice and contacted the mayor, who punted. The mayor did not win the next election, nor did I participate in his further campaigns. As I recall, Mayor Peterson may have been succeeded by former DFL congressman Donald Frazer, who would not have assured access in the first place.

I've sometimes wondered whether it might have been different had the large bozo who addressed the woman he referred to as "Ma," who wore her dirty red coat, pink gloves, and brass knuckles, had said, "Of course, you're free to enter."

When I first became active in political affairs, I held a number of beliefs and biases that gradually have fallen away. When, for example, I participated in local, county, and state conventions, the roles to which I gravitated were as a member and frequently as the chair of the local, county, or a state policy committee. Years later, having been approached on a number of occasions to run for public office, I was approached by the admired Judge Lindsay Arthur and a delegation of several businessmen whose purpose was to persuade me to oppose Senator Humphrey in his pending U.S. senatorial campaign. Their mission conflicted with the conclusion I had reached years earlier, before my civic and political involvement had earned me enough brownie points for them to approach me. Their argument had merit in one respect. While the odds against election do not warrant comment, the peripheral impact of invigorating the Republican Party was their most salient sales point. I told them that I would continue to be active and visible as a businessman in civic and related political matters and issues, but my lifetime decision not to run had been reached years earlier. I indicated I'd be active not as a candidate but as a businessman believing in better government.

Active civic involvement had begun for me in the 1950s, when a group of business leaders in their sixties concluded that Minneapolis should have a Boys Club, modeled on the national organization. They wanted to reach down the socio-economic scale, beyond the levels being addressed by the Boys and Girls Scouts' fine programs, which essentially then attracted middle-class youth.

The YMCA and YWCA were effective also, but there still was the important unfilled niche of poorer youth comprised in part of the children of single-parent minorities (African-Americans and Native Americans) not reached by other programs. I became the youngest Minneapolis businessman to join the Boys Club (now Boys & Girls Clubs) and later spent four years heading this fine outreach but still did not address adequately the needs of the poor.

During the mid-1960s, on the heels of the Los Angeles Watts riots, racial violence swept the country, including Minneapolis. I was approached by a delegation of six clergymen whose purpose was to persuade me to build the next Boys Club in Minneapolis, "on the North Side." Included in the delegation were a Catholic priest (Father Schuler); a Methodist minister, (Rollie Robinson); an Episcopalian minister from south Minneapolis; and the city's foremost Jewish rabbi, who headed the city's largest synagogue, Rabbi Shapiro. My response was an immediate yes.

First, however, we had to jump three hurdles. We needed the approval of the Boys Club board of directors, which was granted in timely fashion. Second, we needed the enthusiastic support of Bert and Gladys Gamble who spoke for the combined Gamble-Skogmo Foundation, which was prepared to fund a Boys Club on the North Side. But a good friend and principal advisor to Bert Gamble cautioned me that whereas the Gambles started their successful enterprise in north Minneapolis, they would be concerned lest the facility in their name, and funded by them, be located in "no-man's land" and be burned down, the fate of a few stores caught up in a night of rioting and burning. We also needed, and this became our major problem, the council's approval of zoning regulations adapted to the specific site.

This was a tall order, as the ward was represented on the council by alderman "Pumpkin Joe" Cohen, and Joe's ward was populated by a large Jewish constituency. The more affluent in the ward were migrating as rapidly as possible to the suburb of St. Louis Park. A number of others were moving out and their population in the area was decreasing, as the population of African-Americans rapidly increased. The small Jewish enterprises were failing.

On my home front, Sally and our family joined me on Saturdays and Sundays in attending the churches and synagogues of the area, and my older kids involved themselves in community volunteer work.

Pumpkin Joe Cohen was pragmatic. "I want to retain my seat on the council. You bring me enough petitions from my ward calling for your damn Boys Club and I'll support rezoning. If not, forget it." My friend, DFL mayor Art Naftlin was highly supportive of the initiative but had noted other problems to face. At his urging much of the wasteland on the North Side was leveled, and with federal funding, converted to low-cost housing. Jews who could afford to move did so and Pumpkin Joe's support weakened.

Meanwhile my civic workload had exploded. For six months, I spent several nights per week in Pumpkin Joe's home territory, meeting with small groups explaining how a Boys Club could be helpful to their area. The ministers, schoolteachers, and school boards helped orchestrate and arrange these small meetings and eventually the alderman's hurdle was cleared. Groundbreaking and construction began.

Unfortunately, the tension of the times continued, mounted, and spread. The head of a local initiator in the epicenter of the hot spot, Syl Davis, and several African-Americans approached me to express two concerns and propose a more relevant and timely initiative. Syl, his wife, and a group of the ardent African-Americans sat down with me and gave their pitch. Whereas the Boys Club would be welcome, the time before it became available delayed its usefulness. Further, the Boys Club itself was a "whitey project." They needed and wanted a facility sooner, where the leadership was black, the kids black, and the work getting the building prepared would involve the kids, black volunteers, and otherwise unemployed labor, and, "You, Whitey, need to help us with sponsorship and business community funding."

That made good sense, and I called a meeting of business leaders, together with DFL mayor Art Naftlin, and we joined forces. Two to three afternoons each week, I drove to the site of The Way building on Olson Highway, parked or double-parked my red Ford, tossed a young black man my car keys, and said, "I'll be back in twenty minutes, and will want and need the keys" to a car I never locked, which was never robbed, taken, or driven. Nor would these young men ever accept a tip. Within a month, the city's business leadership met at The Way, where they maintained quiet while being shouted at, cursed, yet made welcome. The tide was turning, yet we had a long way to go.

Mayor Arthur Naftlin asked me to head the city's Council on Human Relations, a position I accepted. The magnificent caring Jewish lawyer Hy Edelman agreed to work closely with me. (His son met his future bride, an African American from Alabama, at Yale, and their lives have gone on to support equality of opportunity. She became the first African American to pass the bar in Alabama.) The media in the city was superb; one of the several times in a full life I found them to be so. Daily coverage and transparency of the ongoing debates over specific problems between the black and white communities were followed and covered in depth in the news and editorial sections of the Twin Cities' papers.

The FBI, in a state of near alarm, met frequently with me at the time, monitoring closely to see if there were communist connections. J. Edgar Hoover led the FBI during this period, and Senator Joe McCarthy's anti-communist exhortations were anything but helpful. There were, I'm confident, no communist linkages in Minnesota, only human rights and decency. To me, it would not have mattered anyway, for people were the issue, not communism.

"Police brutality" was a popular area of discord, and our local police, headed by Charles Stenvig, police chief, more than adequately represented the "redneck sector" of the citizenry. No doubt it was from them and certain of the trade unions in trucking and construction that Plank-targeted criticism emanated, and these groups gave rise to my first personal death threats. To be on the safe side, I had a hot line to the home of a neighbor policeman, and kept a loaded .38 pistol and a 12-gauge shotgun at bedside.

Fear? I don't think so. I'd known enough fear as a bomber pilot to do other than prepare. It was but an unpleasant aspect of seeking overdue change. The long-term solution to a society in shock and stumbling with discrimination and impediments to equal employment was being actively pursued. Honeywell's CEO, Steve Keating, headed the major businesses' development of the Urban Coalition, and it was on one such evening of a coalition meeting in the auditorium of the region's primary electric utility, Northern States Power, that Steve called for a moment of prayer and silence in the immediate wake of Martin Luther King's assassination that day. Steve had told me before the meeting commenced how he would address it. I told him that would not suffice—and it did not. There was too much shock, grief, anger, and bitterness in the room—chemistry that threatened so much that had been accomplished. I had wanted eulogies and participation by those most hurt, and a postponement of the evening's agenda.

During this era I became interested in the work of the Reverend Leon Sullivan, who led a large, black Philadelphia congregation. He headed a training and motivation center for those underemployed and unemployed. I spent several days with him in Philadelphia, observing his teaching in process and discussing whether Minneapolis minorities and the community might benefit from such a program. Sullivan was enthusiastic and visited Minnesota. Subsequently, the business community utilized the Philadelphia model to form and fund the Twin Cities Opportunities Industrial Center (TCOIC). It took hold with blacks of working age, and for a time, made a contribution. Leon went on to become a great leader and accomplished much.

Apache did substantial program business with General Electric senior executives, one of whom was predisposed within his company agenda to check out Leon Sullivan as a possible director of GE. Virgil Day, a program customer who later became a highly respected Apache board member, had been favorably disposed, and was more so when we discussed my contact with Leon, who accepted board seats on both GE and General Motors.

From Sullivan's perspective, his involvement, he understood, would facilitate employment and help meet some of the opposition of the nation's more reactionary unions. Leon went on to write and promulgate what became known as the Sullivan Principles—guidelines to hiring and employment practices for American businesses operating among the evolving nations of southern Africa.

At this point I want to register my disapproval of the well-intended yet stupid, in my opinion, American college and university student movements calling on American businesses to pull out of South Africa. Involved as I was in heading the University of Minnesota Endowment Fund, and as a trustee of the outstanding Carleton College, located in Northfield, Minnesota, I had more than a ringside seat in the heated controversy. American-based business enterprises were, to my thinking, already positive employer entities in Africa. As a member of the two institutions' investment committees, I believed the student pressure to force the universities and colleges to sell the securities of all American companies doing business in South Africa was counterproductive to the black interests, while annoying to portfolio managers seeking investment performance. While idealistic, the position was dangerously naive.

I was correct in the assumption that the first phase protest would be followed by demands that American companies move out of South African countries. It remains my view that deliberate job destruction would counteract improving living standards, particularly when American manufacturers abroad hold higher standards and ethics than those in the impoverished countries. My volunteering to join the two college presidents in making the pitch to those idealistic, sociological illiterates was declined, both presidents noting it was their responsibility, as indeed it was.

The Minnesota Republican governor, Harold LeVander, reached me in the Houston airport and requested I accept the appointment to head Minnesota's Department of Human Rights. While I was unenthusiastic, my commercial flight had been called and I did not want to be rude to Harold. I also had deep respect for his daughter Jean LeVander's work on political and racial issues and her commitment to civil rights. Well do I recall the phrase that got me—he said, "I would very much enjoy working closely with you on the issues." Unfortunately, Harold attended one meeting, our first, and thereafter sent an observer. Our group, an interesting one, met monthly, but on coming to believe my efforts were being impeded by the governor's neglect, I requested I be replaced.

Years later, how do I feel about the efforts and time commitments to human rights during the heated era of civil rights days? Very good. Satisfied that I'd made a difference important at the time, locally and beyond the horizons of community and the local protagonists. Were the endeavors helpful to Apache's future? Certainly, although not without a price I recognized I was paying. Having founded Apache, the name then most frequently associated with it, in a positive vein, was my own. Respect and credibility, hard often to gain for many, came readily to me, attracting investments both to our program business and to a degree to our shareholder list as well as capital availability. But that's not why I joined the fray. The reason is the title of this memoir.

MEDITATIONS ON MANAGEMENT

I BELIEVE AMERICAN BUSINESS WENT through an era that represented a heyday for "professional management." It was a heyday as well for consultants on the subject, whose livelihoods depend to a large degree on consulting others on managing. Managing involves developing the experience and skills of management, which partakes as much of art and psychology as it can of the various disciplines implied by the adjective professional.

For some years I felt defensive with respect to my self-rating as a professional manager. To my later amusement it seems now to me that I probably managed better than I would have three and four decades ago. What I believe to be most relevant is the adjective professional preceding manager. If professional is omitted from the context of management, it makes a big difference. And whether manager is so prefaced or not, in any such deliberation there are, in my view, two important words relating to management: delegation and participation—delegation without abdication, and participation without floundering in indecision. To await for events to be fully synthesized, or to delay, or to sidestep when anticipation of events and innovation take precedence over being "professional," to me smacks of bureaucracy and poor management.

One tradeoff in my pursuits was my family who needed and warranted more of my time, love, attention, and support. I had time enough to say no, while shortchanging a fine, wonderful wife and mother, with our own discords washing over the lives of our children—who have in aggregate, done very well given their dad's shortcomings, which they have offset increasingly as they matured, by human awareness and respect.

At the same time, I am not the type of person ruefully to reminisce and think, "If only I had done this and hadn't done that." For life is to live, learn, and grow, a recipe that for me is a full, splendid meal and at the core of personal happiness, with a major premise being, as my father put it, "to try to make a very small difference on behalf of others." I leave it to the reader to develop his or her own views on "professional" management. By 2005, the words entrepreneurial and hands-on had largely replaced the more abstract concepts of professional, which to me have more than a tinge of elitist cliché.

John Kocur, who rose to become Apache's president after me and continued for another decade in that position, was a close partner and friend. In 1985, he wrote an introduction to the company's initial history, *Journey into Risk Country*, entitled, "A Short Forward." It is reprinted here because it captures much of the values of the company culture and the spirit continued over many years to be relevant for Apache as for any enterprise wishing to remain vital.

A SHORT FORWARD

In 1984, our company, Apache Corporation, completed its thirtieth year. The following account is but one way of testifying to the effectiveness of Apache employees who have built this company so brilliantly and soundly over the last three decades.

It will be a pleasure to distribute this book to Apache employees; to many thousands of shareholders and participants in various Apache investment programs; to our customers; to our suppliers and consultants; and to all others who are part of the story of our exploration for and development of oil and gas for our country's present and foreseeable energy needs.

But there is one group of potential readers whose names and addresses we do not know, but whose presence—wherever those readers are—is exhilarating.

We salute their dreams and their plans with this book. We hope some copies will pass into their hands, for the story of Apache Corporation is, in truth, a study of continuing entrepreneurship; of risk taken and risk shared; of building respectable and rewarding jobs and careers; of responsibility to land and water resources that have been good to us, not only in our continuing search for petroleum reserves, but in our agricultural and industrial operations as well.

We are heartened by the increasing number of new business starts taking place throughout America. They are being made by men and women who have chosen to journey toward the high country where the maps are usually scarce and the resources usually limited. As one corporation, however, that has traveled that road and chooses to continue on it, we can testify to the quality and sweep of the view once that high country is reached. There is nothing like it anywhere else in life.

Raymond Plank, the co-founder of what is today the Apache Corporation, continues on as chairman and chief executive officer of the organization. His name appears throughout this narrative too many times most probably to please him, and not enough times, in the opinion of myself and others, to identify the immense contribution he has made to the growth, stability, and risk-taking that are identifying features of Apache. I commend to the reader's attention a short statement by Mr. Plank in the closing pages of this history that touches upon the responsibility of a healthy corporation to our country's people, environment and welfare.

I am now of an age where all blessings become more vivid and real. One of these, without question, is the privilege of working in a free society for a company that is intent on making a decent contribution to that society. I wish every reader that same degree of fulfillment.

— John A. Kocur, 1985

John has retired from Apache's management but continues as a respected, contributing and active member of our board and two of its committees, while actively assisting a Florida district judge as a volunteer in public service. The calendar of the 1980s began in Minneapolis and elsewhere with a rush. As usual, however, John Kocur and I were busy both with executing within our areas of responsibility and also planning strategy as far ahead as we believed it productive to plan versus dream.

With John Kocur.

APACHE PETROLEUM COMPANY

THERE ARE BUT TWO WAYS in which the assets of natural resource companies can grow. The first way is straightforward: through discovery and developing added resources commercially to generate profits.

A second—and unique way—would for the sellers of the accretive assets to be able to defer taxes via a tax-free exchange until an actual sale, thus allowing their capital to compound its value. In the second way the unit holder gains direct control of the timing of the sale of all or a portion of the holdings. Apache met these corporate and investor objectives, and the exacting criteria of both the IRS and the SEC. After all, the longer deferred taxes work for creative people, the more the government reaps at the end. (I like to think of that approach as an offset to the overly burdensome excessive consumer spending, credit card society extracting a debilitating toll from America's future.)

John Kocur and I recognized, however, that as the critical mass of Apache-managed assets grew, we would find it increasingly difficult to meet the criteria necessary to allow us to shift tax-deferred mergers into liquid, marketable securities that were publicly traded.

While wrestling with this problem during the mid-1970s, at a time when Apexco operated with investors' assets, we came up with a potential "elegant solution."

If, we reasoned, we could create a publicly owned entity in the form of partnership units rather than stock, we would have an optimum vehicle for investors and Uncle Sam alike. "Uncle" would benefit if, by employing the assets effectively, we were able to create and continue a profitable growing enterprise. The income tax bite would grow, with the government realizing proportionately larger taxes collected if the market value of the liquid assets grew more rapidly than inflation. (The interest rates imposed to restrain inflation had had the opposite effect, leading to accelerated inflation, loss of American purchasing power, and diminished credibility of our government abroad.) On the other hand, the investor could choose to donate his or her appreciated units to qualifying charities at market value. The resultant funding would benefit American charities, which the federal and state taxing authorities deemed in the public interest in the first place.

And the investor would reap tax-advantaged gains and have a tax-free entry into the vehicle, which would also be tradable and liquid.

If we could execute such an exchange, Apache would gain another vehicle of outstanding potential appeal in our pursuit to purchase appropriate assets and value through discovery and development. However, our superb space capsule could not lift off our investors' pad. Both the NYSE and SEC said "No" with more authority than parents normally achieve in greeting the wish lists of their children's compelling wants.

A full five years later, my charming and very bright second wife, Lollie, and I were on an investor trip to Europe's major cities. Our host and arranger was Bill Nicoletti, plus several of his aides from Paine Webber Jackson and Curtis, who had arranged meetings with investor groups. After a long day of investor meetings, Bill, Loll, and I met for a drink in the bar of a Paris hotel to unwind and discuss the next day's agenda. Our talk turned to Apache's earlier rebuff. Bill, who immediately grasped the concept, noted that in the intervening years, regulators had become bolder. He pointed to investment trusts becoming publicly owned, and believed Apache's concept represented an excellent and totally novel vehicle that could now meet with an affirming green light. While somewhat incredulous, and understanding the benefit of new business to his firm (and Bill himself), I authorized him on the spot to make inquiries on our return to the states.

John Kocur was equally incredulous but immediately began a quest among respected U.S. law firms in the interest of selecting one with a "can do, will try" attitude and conviction. He had called on several before meeting with one of the senior partners, Reuben Clark of Wilmer, Cutler and Pickering in Washington, D.C. Reuben was intrigued, thought the concept excellent, and agreed to propose our plan to his partners. As they departed, by then from a bar, Reuben observed to John, "And give my regards to Ray Plank; we were good friends from the class of Yale '44 before the war scattered us to the winds." John did so, his law firm did so, and we were off to the brain-crushing legal and accounting workloads preceding such an undertaking. John Kocur, Reuben, and our in-house attorney, a former SEC branch chief, Mike Valadez, were on the way, as were Bill Nicoletti and his associates, in the design of the first of what came to be labeled by the securities industry as the "master limited partnership" or MLP. Throughout the venture our Chief Financial Officer, Jim Nelson, made a magnificent contribution to our creative endeavor.

As usual within and throughout Apache, we greeted the opportunity with a marked sense of urgency, for during the years since we had started Apexco in 1971, we had been busily piling up reserves, production, and the recurring need for investor liquidity. The legal hurdles to overcome were not monumental, but our internal accountants and public accountants were confronted with difficult accounting and tax reporting requirements.

Because the tax basis of every unit holder's holdings changed with every quarterly distribution, only we at Apache could accurately track the tax basis for every unit holder. (Corporately, the distributions would have been dividends, but here their composition were both returns of capital and perhaps taxable income.) The second variable arose in the price of the units to be traded on the NYSE: because that price would vary daily the calculation of value was exquisitely complex.

Our CFO, Jim Nelson, developed an exclusivity agreement with Arthur Andersen. Jim and his group did a magnificent job developing the computer software programs that were to calculate the investors' tax information. Although the software cost approximately $6 million, licensing agreements with other spellbound Apache emulators recovered our costs in full. Arthur Andersen became the final purchaser of the software package, together with the rights to market the product. Rather than being a startup cash burden to our investors in the newly formed Apache Petroleum Company (APC on the NYSE), our costs had been fully covered up to the point of servicing a rapidly growing owner base. Reuben Clark developed the essential tax opinion, and his firm obtained the requisite IRS ruling. We were in business.

APC proved a highly viable asset acquisition tool, and we were the early robin to carry off the worm to the nest. The market and backers liked the product, and their investors and our unit holders were similarly enthusiastic.

Some lawmakers remained skeptical. Senator William Proxmire of Wisconsin called me before his Senate Committee and posed the logical question:

> "And how many holders of APC units are there, Mr. Plank?"
>
> I responded, "Approximately twenty thousand and growing, Senator."
>
> "That sounds like a lot of partners."

The government's concerns were natural. While investors have long deplored the double taxation of dividends, first as taxable corporate earnings, and again when received by shareholders, the master limited partnerships (MLPs) offered the prospect of making an end play around triple taxation of earnings. Were our vehicle to sweep across corporate America like an unchecked prairie fire, the United States might be in even worse financial condition than it found itself across highly inflationary decades of rapidly growing spending.

For several years, our MLP was of utmost significance to our successful pursuit of Apache critical mass. It was, for a time, a superb acquisition vehicle, as the owners received cash distributions from their units that were to a large degree a return of capital and therefore available upon receipt for investment—job-creating investment in the private sector versus government bureaucracy.

There were three primary potential markets for Apache Pe-

*Apache Corporation's 1970s logo and that of its
subsidary, Apache Petroleum Company (APC).*

troleum Company's units. The first was for and among Apache
program investors who exchanged their program units into
$20.00 partnership units on the basis of a tax-free exchange.

Generally, the holders of our drilling program units had, before the exchange, written off and deducted against other income, or oil-run income, the allowable tax deductions to the
point where their basis for tax purposes in the per units held
was between 50¢ and perhaps $3 per unit. If Apache as general
partner neither drilled for more hydrocarbons nor acquired additional assets on behalf of the partnership, the underlying value of their units would have declined as the depleting reserves
were produced.

If, on the other hand APC made cash distributions, and
drilled for and acquired additional assets, the units would have
a potential growth dimension. Further, without a growth component, the APC units would probably have sold at a discount
to true value, versus at some premium to carrying value as a
potential growth vehicle with tax benefits built in. It was important that APC have growth potential to provide our original
unit holders appreciation in addition to liquidity. Backed with

the new MLP, Apache and APC continued to pursue growth.

Some corporations, such as Dow Chemical, had decided to sell off significant portions of their gas production and to acquire a larger percentage of their feed stocks in the competitive purchase market. Their sophistication gave them a competitive edge. When I sat down with their CEO at their headquarters in Midland, Michigan, he was quick to grasp the potential benefits to Dow's shareholders, as evidenced by his calling to the discussion his very able chief financial officer.

Apache and Dow in the early 1980s concluded Apache's largest asset acquisition on behalf of APC, a transaction built around the exchange of units and incorporating several innovations. By accepting units for a significant percentage of a potentially attractive investment vehicle, Dow gained control of the timing of their sales consistent with meeting their own needs and objectives. They also might experience appreciation of the units they accepted when and if they sold.

The Dow relationship and transaction were of enormous benefit. Our little IPO units responded by climbing in the marketplace from $20 per unit into the high twenties, well before the high-tech craze soared in the 1990s.

Most markets, in my experience, rarely pause and stabilize where rationality might suggest they should. Understanding this, several of our directors, John Kocur, and I began to see the handwriting on the wall, even as market euphoria continued. We began to note that some brokerage representatives were selling their clients units on the basis of their being a tax-sheltered, high-yield, and relatively secure asset. Whoops! The distributions were to a significant degree a return of the investors' capital; the more the buyer paid for his units, the lower the return on capital and the less the percentage attributable to yield.

The second major factor was the degree to which the price

volatility of oil and gas could wreak havoc on the ability of any oil and gas MLP to generate cash distributions in declining phases of the price cycle. Another extraordinary disruption to the price cycle was exacerbated by the destruction of long-term gas contracts in favor of month-to-month and daily gas sales, which, by the way, temporarily enriched Enron and its nine principal middleman competitors—all of whom fell from favor, but only one of which, Enron, has been prosecuted.

There is a section in Apache's fifty-year history, *Critical Mass: Apache at 50*, which deals with the subject as perceived and written by Apache's very able David Higgins:

> Apache Petroleum Company, at one time larger than Apache Corporation itself, was doomed by commodity-price collapse, the resultant reduction in investor distributions and 1986 tax-law reform. Structured to provide its investors flexibility through liquidity, tax shelter, annual cash flow and the potential for growth through exploration, development, acquisition and market appreciation, it couldn't survive the combined weight of less-attractive, and ultimately phased-out, tax advantages in a period of low commodity prices.

Apache, mindful of the above, was the first to create and enter the MLP field—and the first to leave it. As oil and gas prices fell in 1986 in short months from $26.50 to $10 per barrel, there was great damage to the United States and to its upstream energy producers. I would note, however, that the MLP has found a place in the widening investment spectrum less unsuitable than in markets subject to price deterioration than natural gas, which carries the unique distinction of top volatility among commodities. When that phenomenon is paired with free market rhetoric, coupled with the lack of effective regulation by Congress, causes and remedies are ignored to the detriment of our nation.

In the mid-1980s.

Where the larger MLP opportunities have been found is in depreciating assets such as commercial real estate, pipelines, and companies whose revenues are tied to rents paid as transportation fees rather than to the commodities transported. Apache exited the MLP arena in the same era when tax changes rendered public drilling programs a much less desirable investment vehicle. We did so by offering our APC unit holders two options in addition to that provided by the market: They could elect to exchange APC units for shares of stock in a new company, Key Exploration, on the basis of a tax-free exchange. Or Apache would acquire their units through a taxable exchange with Apache shares. They did both; some investors allocated a portion of their holdings to each. Many who elected to accept Apache shares had acquired them while the price was rising, thus allowing these investors to mitigate their losses.

David Higgins, Director, Public Affairs and investor ombudsman.

Others took their holdings to Key, run by Apache's former president, Mick Merelli. Mick had retired from Apache, choosing to remain in Denver rather than move to Houston in 1992. He eliminated for a period the payout, and built the company and its market value through good drilling decisions and acquisitions. Mick is a wise and able executive.

In dropping our annual program sales after 1986, Apache continued to manage the assets of those who had not exchanged, plus the interests of the 1984 Shell Offshore Program, the largest program ever formed by Apache. Even in 2008, it continued to produce revenues, returning $5,500 per unit in its twenty-fourth year. The offshore program holders had benefited from additional finds Apache made on the acreage originally acquired.

The master limited partnership had clearly proven its usefulness to Apache and would go on to do so for many businesses.

MANAGING TRANSITION

BEHIND EVERY SIGNIFICANT LIFE TRANSITION there usually is some form of a personal phase spent building toward
longer-range goals. My first transition occurred during the several month-period prior to the decision to exit the small yet
unique bookkeeping, accounting, and tax practice I had started
with Brooks Fields upon college graduation in June 1946. At
that time I was asked to take on the responsibility of managing
the oil and gas properties in which a number of high-income
investors had been defrauded by two sets of unscrupulous promoters bent on making quick bucks through kickbacks from
drilling service companies—something I exposed by conduct-
ing personal audits of their records. I was told at an investor
meeting that they wanted me to represent their interests. They
would fire the promoter operators immediately following the
meeting. At the time, I suggested we would be pleased to work
with them to locate and retain operators above reproach, but
they strongly preferred that we take over. I agreed to present a
comprehensive strategic plan, provided we had several months
to research and develop the preferred alternative.

During that time I concentrated on what could be achieved in the first five years. Behind those objectives were hopes and a dream, too far in the future to surface before my associates and I could put together our plan for presentation. Recognizing my utter lack of qualifications, I did not deem it relevant or appropriate to talk about dreams; there were obstacles along the route that needed to be surmounted, not to mention the risks of being perceived and proven to be an idiot, before the foal of the future horse had gained body to match its long legs. My plan was enthusiastically approved on the basis of its achievable shorter-term goals.

There were, and I believe are, almost invariably principles relevant to long-term achievement worth identifying early and remembering throughout the long climb up the mountain. Those principles transcend the question of whether the entity with which one identifies is privately or publicly owned, the latter being the essential framework for the vehicle we fashioned because the capital required exceeded our financial capacity.

The use of investor capital requires a high standard of integrity. That, for me, was an easy principle ingrained by both my parents, accompanied by a strong work ethic, the importance of savings, and an appreciation of the fiduciary role that decision makers bear to those who empower them. As I plagiarized from someone along life's trail, "One who thinks solely of self is soon forgotten; those who care about others, live on."

I believed before starting Apache Corporation that it would be vital for our program investors to be provided with alternatives, according to their needs and desires. We chose to pursue this principle, versus one that could have produced conflict. Conflict is inevitable but resolution is more likely achieved when players seek advancement of the whole versus self-aggrandizement—this truth is inherent in the decline and fall of so-called civilizations and is a constant throughout recorded history.

The pursuit of lifetime learning becomes relevant as a means of the advancement of self and indeed mankind around the globe. Or, as my father said, "Follow the straight and narrow path" and "Know the difference between right and wrong."

My parents' teachings, and my having been surrounded by death during preparation for and service as a combat bomber pilot in World War II, resulted in an objective I identified and pursued since transitioning from war and college graduation. I wanted to create a successful business to serve as a platform to facilitate outreach to others less fortunate than I. In both my upbringing and my having survived the war, my considered choice between piling up money while deferring personal gain, or lining up my objectives as I "made my way," was a simple one. I would pursue both interests simultaneously, would live my approach, and would teach it in the belief of its positive impact upon others.

My outreach efforts served our corporate obligations well, appealing both to our internal corporate culture among employee families, as well as counterbalancing the negative public perceptions of the consistently maligned "oil business." Rather than making passive dollar contributions to worthy causes, I would personally seek to make a small difference, with the majority of our money invested in innovative programs to which my commitment was time and personal involvement, principally in education and health. The internal impact on employee families was immense as our employees embraced these principles.

My rules for self were and are:

- First, never ask for a financial contribution, be it for a social or a political cause, without first having contributed personally.

- Second, during the early formative years of a new program at my initiative, carry the startup costs personally until the program has taken roots. For me, this included avoiding going to Apache for support or financial help prior to demonstrated success.

- Third, do not seek federal government financing; private sector initiative trumps federal bureaucracy and control, particularly in the formative years. Tax deductibility constitutes sufficient incentive and is invariably less wasteful of federal dollars.

THE MOVE TO DENVER

APACHE'S LAST FULL YEAR IN Minneapolis, 1986, was momentous in light of two undertakings and their impact on the future: the acquisition of oil and gas assets from Armand Hammer's publicly owned conglomerate, Occidental Petroleum ('Oxy'), and the decision to move the company's headquarters to Denver.

Oxy was bent on being a not-so-friendly "white knight" to another independent as Hammer's appetite was then focused on expanding his own petrochemical operations in the Southwest. The assets Apache particularly coveted were largely in Oklahoma and west Texas, with a smattering in the Gulf of Mexico and Louisiana. Marvin Davis, whom I came to know well in Minneapolis, was a neighbor to Armand Hammer in Beverly Hills, and knew Armand much better than I. Until the last moment, Marvin planned to purchase half of Oxy's undivided interests should we reach agreement. Marvin was a marvelous intermediary who enjoyed working both with our able corporate development director, Jim Kneser, and with me. As fate would have it, days before the negotiated purchase was to close, commodity prices of oil and gas hit bottom. Marvin told me he would prefer not to go back that heavily into the oil business, and if we agreed to close the purchase, he would transfer his loan agreement to Apache and give Apache the better part of a year to get him off the debt agreement.

Knowing our own creditors and the rating agencies would consider the move rash, I contacted John Kocur and Charlie Hahn to see if they believed we could quickly raise the money directly from insurance companies and pension funds, several of whom had worked with us in the financing associated with the Shell Oil Offshore Drilling Program, and of which David Higgins, who had been valuable with Apache, was equity investor ombudsman for years in close contact with operation partner Shell. All three thought we could raise the funds necessary and our decision, which included verbal board approval, allowed us to go forward within twenty-four hours.

We were moving headquarters to Denver and nearing completion of the Oxy acquisition when Mick Merelli and Steve Farris joined Apache. Mick replaced John Kocur as president, enabling John to retire while remaining a valued Apache director and confidant during my Apache career.

Leaving our Minnesota headquarters posed its own challenges but moving headquarters to Denver proved to be a milestone for Apache. Our new incarnation required that we achieve a substantially greater level of critical mass to operate as an oil company dependent on internally generated cash flow from wells we owned and operated for our own account, than when we derived most of our cash from small net-revenue interests shared with investor programs. That strategic decision shifted our primary focus from drilling to the acquisition of assets with upside potential via "acquire and exploit" tactics.

Marvin Davis and I sign papers on our $440 million purchase from Occidental Petroleum.

Rather than seek acquisitions from smaller companies in the popular auction market, purchased in exchange for shares, we would acquire assets for cash taxable to the sellers. This dictated that we shift our strategy temporarily to debt, and our debt ratio would inevitably rise. Funding would also come from primarily issuing shares in the market at a premium price to their asset value, to which our growth strategy and value-added performance was intended to have market appeal to investment firm customers. We needed, in a cyclical oil market, to catch the cycle at an early point of advancing commodity prices versus the inevitable latter phases of cyclical decline.

We needed also to purchase asset packages from larger oil companies as the major integrated oil companies would be willing to sell as they sought cost reduction and cash redeployment in their quest for larger reserves in lesser drilled basins of the world fit their strategic priorities.

The self-interest of the investment bankers had long been to promote auction sales, pointing to their likelihood of finding a buyer in behalf of the client seller, who for one reason or other would pay a larger premium above asset value for its own reasons, to which the investment bankers added two more reasons: perhaps it could entice the strongest bids into a bidding war, and an auction would best assure a board of directors that it was getting top price.

Apache countered these arguments by noting that we would pay a fair and favorable price, that the sophisticated seller knew the value of oil and gas assets, and that we should be allowed to make the first bid on a highly confidential basis, before those assets went to the auction market. If we failed to make an acceptable bid, then they could always proceed to auction.

We were passionate in our belief that upon studying assets of the majors closely, we might come up with situations in which both our independent engineers and internal people would find certain properties in areas of our expertise that would afford greater upside potential. Our clincher was twofold and one line of reason held special appeal: We could and would evaluate and act quickly, thus avoiding potentially severe internal morale problems among employees and their families. Either the sellers or we would wish to retain people constructive to our future within our growing company. Thus we came to change the traditional ways in which asset purchases were made, to spur our growth and meet both sellers' and buyers' objectives.

Such was the case in the 1991 acquisition from Amoco (now British Petroleum). Amoco's investment banker, Morgan Stanley, sought a foreign buyer in pursuit of asset representation in the world's largest market. Unfortunately for Amoco, the investment banker search dragged on while we diligently analyzed production data and fields, the performance of which was publicly reported. Amoco's acquired properties were largely oil, while in North America, by drilling we were finding over 80 percent natural gas and sought a closer balance within the two distinct oil and gas markets.

Doubling Apache's assets and balancing our oil and gas base, the Amoco acquisition fed our critical mass objective as we also sold equity to keep our debt in line. This was consistent with the goal of pursuing larger wells and fields internationally, while increasing our North American drilling (both to exploit leaseholds acquired coincident to asset purchases and to expand our North American lease-hold base per se).

Having committed to banks and the investing public to reduce our debt ratios from the near 70 percent to 50 percent within a year, we pursued three strategies concurrently.

We decided within days, however, that prudence dictated we sell off our Rocky Mountain assets as rapidly as possible, except for two wells in Nevada reputed then to have recoverable oil of 11 million barrels, leaving 3 or 4 million more proven barrels to produce. (These two wells continued to produce beyond the 20 million barrels we recovered before we parted company with them!)

Our approach was much more conservative than that of our competitors. During our Denver years and beyond, many competitors acquired properties remote from existing production in the interest of impressing the stock market with production growth. Costs associated with distance rise more rapidly than revenues, unless buoyed by price increases in an industry that is both cyclical and competitive. I had tracked the industry over many decades until I could anticipate reverses.

DENVER POLITICS
AND PASTIMES

IN PREPARING TO MOVE APACHE headquarters, I had made the erroneous assumption that a relatively small oil company, though well-known and well-regarded in Minnesota, would cast a relatively small shadow on moving to Denver where oil companies, a few of them large, had regional offices and where smaller entities abounded. Colorado governor Roy Romer changed that by pounding on his Democrat political chest, and Denver mayor Federico Peña was quick to follow.

Roy Romer came to call on me at our Minneapolis offices and chose to interpret Apache's pending move as a large turkey feather to adorn his fedora. Both Roy and Federico quickly requested I serve on committees comprised in part of businessmen. I accepted one committee appointment from each, for a relatively short period, thinking I might add to existing relationships while possibly adding some value to deliberations as had been afforded in Minneapolis. Both of these men had a remarkable propensity for lecturing their audience and little interest in dialogue except at social gatherings, where both were affable hosts.

It was not necessary, however, that I withdraw in turtle fashion. Lewis Sharp, formerly with the Metropolitan Museum of Art, and other members of his board encouraged me to join the board of the Denver Art Museum, which I did for two reasons. Years earlier I had founded the Ucross Foundation in Wyoming to support the arts and sponsor an artists-in-residence colony. The highest and best use of its restored, historic buildings has proven itself through the long-term impact of literature, visual art, music and dance, all produced by Ucross residents.. I welcomed closer ties to the arts when I moved to Denver. They were easier to pursue than from Minneapolis, 1,050 miles removed. (I also appreciated the fact that my Wyoming second home was 411 miles from my Denver apartment.)

I also took a more active role in industry affairs and became better acquainted with Colorado Democrat senator Tim Wirth, whom I'd known and respected while in Minnesota. Making it a point to attend as many of Senator Wirth's constituent luncheons as possible, and finding him highly rational, I had no problem with his environmental bent. At one candid luncheon, he said he hoped to ride the environmental horse into the White House. Believing him balanced in his approach, I think I applauded as lustily as his longtime supporters.

From Denver I also became very active in industry matters at a personal level, having come to conclude the well-known and frequently quoted industry source, the Independent Petroleum Association of America (IPAA) was a hunting dog that didn't hunt or serve the energy policy issues either at large or specific to the course of its membership at the national level. Fortunately, the state-affiliated associations, unlike the national organization, which I regarded as more of a social club, were much more effective and carried their load remarkably well. Also in Denver I was asked to serve on the National Petroleum

Council. From my perspective I could contribute little relative to the real work spearheaded by scientists and managers from the major oil companies, but the organization held my interest and membership for several years.

Together with several very bright Wyoming young men, we founded American Energy Assurance Council (AEAC) an organization headed by John Jenkins that held its conferences in Ucross, Wyoming, focusing on national security policy. I contacted governors from oil- and gas-producing states interested in energy policy, a topic over which potential and regional gridlock has prevailed for well over forty years. The governors of Wyoming, Colorado, Utah, Oklahoma, and Texas worked closely with us, while North Dakota's Democratic governor, George Sinner, became our chairman. They worked closely with their state's senators and representative members and Apache's growing constituency of royalty owners. These latter, eventually numbering more than ten thousand recipients of periodic royalty checks, were to confer on me their highest award, an honorary plaque that I continue to value highly.

To me, John Jenkins, Executive Director of AEAC, rose to the highest level of personal effectiveness of his career in so far as I have followed him. He recruited not only automobile company support but that of major foundations from the West Coast (Hewlett Packard), to Illinois, New York, and elsewhere, and raised funds in excess of $5 million to carry on the work of AEAC's public education activities. We were also supported financially by the Army, Navy, Department of Commerce, and industry at large, to whom energy availability at affordable costs was relevant.

I remained on the project while Admiral James Watkins chaired the Department of Energy. An incident in Washington led us to abort the project, however. President George

H. W. Bush's chief of staff, John Sununu, joined a meeting in Washington with George Sinner (co-chair of AEAC), Admiral Watkins, and John Jenkins. Sununu did not agree with Admiral Watkins, and tempers flared. As Admiral Watkins rose to leave the meeting, Sununu yelled at him to sit down, to which Watkins retorted, "Go f—yourself." Concluding that our initiative had seen its finest hour and concluding President George H. W. Bush and his senior staff were singing from the same hymnal, we folded our wings and parachuted to ground zero, in time to pursue related energy issues another day—and in this context ultimately from Houston as well as Denver.

This may be a good a place to comment on my exposure to relationships with the Bush family. The oldest son of Republican senator Prescott Bush and I were fellow classmates and acquaintances at Yale University. In college I was well aware that his next-oldest brother, George H. W. Bush. had gone directly into the navy from high school and served in the Pacific theater as a dive bomber pilot. (There are accounts of his exploits and bravery both in the books *Flyboys* by James Bradley and *The Greatest Generation* by Tom Brokaw—the former, I found fascinating; the latter, interesting.)

Upon returning from overseas, which George H.W. was lucky to do given his close calls, he went to Yale, where one of his roommates was Thomas Stroock from Casper, Wyoming. Stroock became successful in the Rocky Mountain quest for oil. George H.W. Bush also developed a drilling company while pursuing public service and a political career. He eventually utilized his extensive contact base to raise money for Hugh Liedtke, the CEO of Pennzoil, which eventually won the lawsuit that sent Texaco into bankruptcy. The successful litigator on behalf of Pennzoil was Joe Jamail; in Houston he would later be my personal attorney. When Pennzoil sold to Shell, Joe moved his Gulfstream IV to hangar it with Apache's plane. Given this coincidence, Joe Jamail and I were to become friends.

I first met George H.W. when he came to St. Paul, Minnesota, in 1978 at my request to campaign on behalf of my good friend, Al Quie, then running for governor. Quie had served in the House of Representatives for twenty years when Gene Trumble, head of Apache's public affairs, and I took on the role of heading his fund-raising, succeeding his previous First District chairman, whose contacts beyond the First District were limited. George H.W. and I came to know each other on a first-name basis during what came to be dubbed the Minnesota Miracle (Minnesota's Republicans carried both senatorial seats—one regular term, the other a replacement. Not only was Al Quie elected governor and both senatorial seats won, but Republicans elected five of the eight members to the House of Representatives, with majorities in the State House and State Senate).

While George H. W. lost the nomination to the presidency, he became the vice presidential nominee with Ronald Reagan. Minnesota, home of the Democrat Farm Labor Party, is among the most far left states of the country. Personally, although I have enjoyed working with a number of Democrats on issues extending beyond oil and gas, when it comes to the use of the word liberal, the adjective seems more applicable to their propensity to be liberal with other people's money through its collection and disbursement.

Papa George had, concurrent with his business undertaking, advanced to head the Central Intelligence Agency and spent duty service in China, which his brother Prescott capitalized on by identifying and attracting capital for Chinese investment. His middle son, Jeb Bush, followed the political track to become

Florida's governor on the Republican ticket. For a period, the Democrats wailed that it was important to pull the rug out from under the Bush family, lest they establish a Bush dynasty. Not to worry; George W. and Jeb stubbed their own toes. George H. W., who reached the pinnacle of public approval in Desert Storm One, won with UN support and with most of the costs of the lightning-like victory picked up by other nations (at the behest of secretary of state Jim Baker of Texas and secretary of defense Dick Cheney, my Wyoming respected friend for many years).

When it came to election time in 1992 and the attendant public debates, George H. W. had a favorable public poll rating of 70 percent, which was sinking, however, as an economic downturn ensued. I well recall the "staged" debate among three contenders, President Bush, Bill Clinton, and Ross Perot. President Bush consulted his wristwatch three times in front of tens of millions of Americans, as my heart sank, and I wondered if he really wanted to return to the White House.

While I thought Ross Perot lacked political depth, he did make good use of the "bully pulpit," and through his use of charts was probably best at reaching the audience.

I did appreciate a senior Perot campaign handler who asked me to draft an energy policy proposal, the absence of which I had lamented for three decades. I spent close to three days and nights on that assignment, but Ross made his first withdrawal from the race, saying that he and his family were tired of the death threats. He turned on and off again, and my time spent was a good exercise, but the concepts went ungraded—nothing new there. The United States seems bent on shooting from the hip.

George's son Neil and I met in Denver, where he served on the board of Silverado Savings and Loan, which made loans to real estate developers, some of whom were investors in Neil's foray into Argentina, as a place to find oil and his future. His geologists' undertakings, typical of neophytes, met with failure.

The friendly Neil Bush and I both shopped at the same Denver grocery store. A few blocks away lived then Democratic governor Roy Romer, a father of eight with a voracious appetite, which led to a confession hot on the heels of denial of an affair. Whereupon he took his "family values" (à la Clinton), first to Washington and then to California, where his trail ends for me in smog.

HOUSTON YEARS—CIRCLING THE WAGONS

WHEN ASKED, "WHY DID YOU move from Denver to Houston?" I occasionally quipped, "We moved to Houston to circle the wagons"—to be at the center of the global oil business and to consolidate our holdings and our standing as an important, innovative producer. Apache's axis had begun to shift to the south and southwest, first with the Oxy acquisition, then with Amoco. As with Denver, we had intended to consolidate our acquired oil and gas properties, and our drilling along the coast and in the Gulf of Mexico, and many fields westward in the Permian Basin of west Texas. These had been run for a number of years out of Tulsa, where we had grown rapidly in our large base acreage position in the Anadarko Basin of western Oklahoma and where John Black, our expert oil finder, had hit several home runs that propelled Apache forward even as we moved to Denver in 1987.

Houston is the widely acknowledged "oil capital of the world" and most of its senior decision makers and many highly trained professional experts—which included geologists, geophysicists, petroleum engineers, and energy-wise law and accounting firms—were close at hand, within lunch and dinner range, versus at jet-flight distances. Wall Street is also very well represented with senior people minutes versus hours away.

Major energy service companies and drilling companies with extensive international operations and senior staffing are also nearby and very helpful to our operations people, while the area's workforce is advanced by universities of high stature, including Rice University, the University of Texas, Texas A&M, the University of Houston, and Baylor, among others. Medical facilities in Houston are top of the line, though often choked up, due to its being the nation's fourth largest city as well as attracting patients worldwide.

The city is big on philanthropy—it supports the arts and sciences. Roger Plank has served as president of the Alley Theatre, which has connections with the Ucross Foundation.

Perhaps the major positive is the energy, commitment, initiative, and attitude of the people—there is an innovative, gung ho, can-do, "Let's get on with it" attitude. Houston is very much alive, contagiously so. As the automobile plates frames proclaim, "Don't Mess with Texas."

It did take me a few years in Houston to get past the loss of the presidential election to Bill Clinton. In Houston, while it was business first, George H. W. has remained a popular speaker and a very good man. We met again at each of two years' events in behalf of the preservation of wartime aircraft. He addresses me as "Ray"; I was comfortable rejoining, "Mr. President." We also shot quail together on two annual occasions in south Texas, when the season is moist enough for quail to abound.

Apache's stockholder value swelled and dividend payouts tagged along well for a growth company, which normally prefers appreciation through production increases to higher dividend payouts. Apache delivered both and our then chief financial officer, Roger Plank, and treasurer Matt Dundrea moved our debt ratio down over several years into the 30-plus percentile with smiles from myself and our soon-to-be president and chief operating officer Steve Farris.

As Apache executed our move to Houston, the strategic pursuit of critical mass continued. We were beginning to close the gap between cash flow internally generated and long-term capital investments both domestically and abroad. But we weren't there yet. Approximately $600 million worth of Texaco assets —largely in Texas—were to come first. Texaco had planned to auction off a chunk of neglected assets and had brought the very able Clarence Cazalot back from abroad to "tidy up" its U.S. holdings. While Jim Kneser joined Marvin Davis as then head of corporate development, it was Jim Bauman, who had moved to Houston from Wyoming and Denver, who first got wind of Texaco's intentions. I paddled off to White Plains, New York, to become acquainted with Texaco's chief financial officer, an IBM veteran.

Within 20 miles of my Ucross, Wyoming home, lived John McKinley, the retired CEO of Texaco. I had sat next to him at the head table when John was guest speaker to a large Houston audience. I had also visited with John at a pheasant and duck shoot paradise equidistant from White Plains and New York City, so I knew him to be an ardent pheasant hunter. I invited John to Ucross on several occasions to join me pheasant shooting, and interestingly enough on Christmas Day of 1992, after shooting birds together, he joined me for Christmas lunch at my Ucross home shortly after dropping his hunting glasses, which we were unable to locate on that cold, beautiful Christmas day shoot. (Nor was my beloved chocolate Labrador retriever, Hershey Bar, attuned to the scent of hunting glasses.)

As a frequent guest at the McKinley home, I asked him one weekend evening whether he maintained contact with headquarters, to which his response was, "I talk to White Plains every weekday." He had a good herd of cattle; I had ridden over his ranch and noted various groups of his mostly Black Angus herd. He told me he'd be selling off his spring-born heifers that year. I said that since we had gone from managing directly our herd to a tenant rancher, it would no longer be a conflict of interest were I to purchase some thirty head with our tenant rancher to run for me, as he did for others. John realized he'd made a good sale and by then he knew we were interested in purchasing the oil and gas properties in a negotiated transaction.

With the rail laid with McKinley, Steve Farris and I called on Clarence Cazalot in his Houston office, who had been well briefed on Apache by our corporate development number two, George Solich. Steve Farris and I found Cazalot very open, with an in-depth knowledge of Apache.

It's important to note that when important changes are in the offing, oil company foremen and field hands sense what's coming, and with their families, become concerned with respect to their future job security. Word had begun to get around, and with Apache approaching Texaco on a top-down basis, Texaco, also concerned for its operations people, cooperated with Steve's operations personnel. This enabled both parties to evaluate both physical and human assets concurrently.

Apache involved our people at multiple levels. For several weeks, they spent weekdays in the field, inspecting the physical

Another day at the salt mines.

assets; on weekends, a number of the Texaco employees met on their time with our senior people in our offices to further evaluate assets and personnel. Because Apache always sought upside potential opportunities and possible field extensions, Steve recognized the importance of identifying and developing a plan of exploitation beforehand to get off to a fast start, to reverse the normal oil field decline rate of the assets by growing production above previously anticipated decline curves.

Once large international companies have developed their fields, some focus increasing attention on new, virgin opportunities in a worldwide portfolio. Concurrently, to reduce their costs as fields deplete, they limit exploitation expenditures. When field hands and their foreman must pursue this process, the loss of time combined with low level of authority can create frustration and bitterness from the same people the business relies upon for profitable field production. Some majors, such as Shell and Exxon Mobil, maintain their fields at higher efficiency levels than others, having a better level of employee respect in their corporate culture.

With Steve's planning, on the day in 1994 when Apache took over the Texaco well operations, a hundred service provider trucks were on the road to upgrade specific wells. The field hands and their foremen loved it, and their performance proved the point. We were able quickly to reduce production declines and generate a higher rate of return on our assets employed.

Announcing the deal, I received a normal call from an alert *Wall Street Journal* reporter who inquired why we expected to make good money on older Texaco properties that had been producing for years. I replied, "Well, we're a bit like pigs following cows through a cornfield. The scraps are pretty good for a company with our particular strategy." That must have been understood, for I received over a hundred miniature pigs in my office, including two Steuben Glass little piglets, one from Clarence Cazalot, who later became head of Marathon Oil. Clarence had noted he'd not been a farm boy and quickly learned from one of his people about pigs following cattle. We had T-shirts and lightweight Texaco "red star" pig jackets made, which many of the Texaco people hung on their walls or wore. Our industry takes enough flak from the politicians, "earth warmers," and motorists outraged when gasoline prices soar, that the jags of humor shared became welcome levity.

We had not long been in Houston before ConocoPhillips's

CEO, Jim Mulva, with whom Steve Farris became well acquainted, let us know that he was interested in getting debt down by year-end balance sheet time. Steve acquired a number of properties from him in northern Canada, largely in an area called Zama. From start to closing, that approximately $350 million deal required only ninety days. Two men of the Alberta far north, Al Buron and Roger Harrison, did a fine job of raising production above planned decline curves in a daunting area that limits remedial drilling and building gathering lines until the permafrost enables movement—and then with the hazard of winter temperatures of fifty degrees below zero.

Until we moved from Denver to Houston, Steve Farris's career experience had been solely in North America. Egypt and Australia had been outside his involvement. Foreign exploration and production had become of great importance to Apache as we rotated foreign postings. Steve's interest in foreign opportunities was vital to the growth of the company prior to his planned ascendancy to CEO. During this interval we spent a great deal of time together. His travel schedule was brutal and our informal luncheon discussions helped close the gap. His very able and ambitious executive assistant, Vicki Miller, made it her practice to reach her desk by 6:30 a.m., at which time she organized Steve's priorities, papers, and agenda for the day.

Both Steve and I pursued an open-door policy, and over several years our open door meant "enter," and people did. If their topics were relevant to areas in which we were in transition, I would remain. If otherwise and our discussions were complete, I would depart for my office. If I was called away for important phone calls from persons I'd been seeking to reach, my wonderful assistant, Irene Lueckemeyer, would come for me and I would depart to take the call. By my eightieth birthday, Apache's board and I were ready for Farris to become CEO, which was announced at our May 2002 annual meeting.

GULF of MEXICO and the SHELL PARTNERSHIP

APACHE'S INITIATION TO THE GULF of Mexico stemmed from the early years of Ted Bartling's reign from 1955 to 1966 as Apache's executive vice president overseeing exploration and production.

We were attracted to the Gulf for two reasons. First, it produced approximately 25 percent of U.S. domestic natural gas and oil and high gravity condensate from highly porous rock formations, largely from shallow water depths, laid down over the millions of years by the Mississippi River. These high-flowing wells were from multiple sediments, in over twenty formations, mostly offshore Louisiana. Also, we wanted to bring forward the Gulf of Mexico as an important region in Apache's portfolio because Gulf gas prices were the highest in North America, served by robust pipelines to major population centers.

Ted Bartling had won quick executive and board approval to open a Lafayette, Louisiana, office and then people it with oil finders and a skeleton crew of competent engineers who also served our South Coast operations. He moved Reid French and several others to establish our presence, reasoning that the lesser-drilled offshore Texas should also host fields of size as in offshore Louisiana. We hunted and pecked without offshore discoveries, while the office earned bread-and-butter money onshore in south Texas, whose formations also extended south into the relatively shallow state waters and beyond.

Reid French contributed his greatest service to Apache when he noted that Shell Offshore, which operated a drilling exploration partnership, was about to lose a partner, Bechtel, which was withdrawing from further exploration. He recommended we seek to replace them by joining the Shell partnership in Bechtel's stead. We formed our own Shell Offshore Partnership to which I appointed David Higgins to be participant ombudsman, representing the interests of the limited partners. To be certain that we offered equity participation to those who qualified as sophisticated investors, we set the investment minimums at $150,000 per unit, collectible over several years as the funds might be required.

Wanting funds for acreage that Shell would lease at auction sales by the Minerals Management arm of the federal government, and for the equity investors to accept the tax-deductible dry hole and noncommercial well risks, we developed two added separate funds we believed suitable to institutional investors. One would pay for the depreciable assets—pipe, tubing, and connecting short lines to the larger pipeline intersections—with the other paying the acreage costs. This combination was known as "functional allocation."

At the time, Shell was known and regarded by many to be the master of the Gulf offshore, which was referenced by some as "the Shell Lake." With Shell as operator, our products were the only investor product in the United States with which suitable investors could participate with Shell. While price cycles were to buffet the partnerships, particularly as Shell was leasing at prices at cyclical peak, our internal sales force had a field day.

As we also sold our programs through our "wholesale sales group," the large investment firms held back, as their sales forces realized their larger investors would be tying up money, often taken out of the corporate securities market, for a period of five or more years. Although late in executing selling agreements, our internal salespeople were beginning to be approached by investors wanting in, and on top of having funds withdrawn from their wealthier clients, the large investment firms were missing "a kick at the can." We quickly raised $600 million in commitments to three funds. Shell ceased its uneasiness over the creditworthiness of our endeavor as it realized the money was at hand. Six hundred million dollars proved more than enough to carry our share, and we did not call for the final 40 percent of the funds.

Although the offshore investor partnership was no blazing financial success for the institutional investor in equipment, surprisingly the highest risk investors did pretty well, and the unanticipated consequences benefited Apache shareholders and the growth of the corporation beyond the expectations at the outset.

In small and moderate-size oil and gas fields, lofty initial production rates usually decline rapidly. Single-formation permeable oil wells often become uneconomic at lower production rates within the first five years; a large portion of the well's productive life can be whipsawed by cyclical price downturns in this short period. In our offshore program, however, due to numerous productive zones in several of our Shell-leased fields, and additionally found production on our 5,000- to 5,500-acre tracts, the program didn't go uneconomic until its twenty-seventh year!

Many of our investors have either died or are in their eighties to early nineties, their holdings having been transferred to their heirs who benefited from semiannual payouts. Apache recognized when the exploration and drilling phase was over, and we released the equity participants from further contractual calls for funding, while David Higgins continued to represent their interests and was responsible for communications until his retirement from Apache in late 2009. Because Apache as general partner had the right to participate in future acquired lands, we converted a portion of the cash flow on right-of-refusal lands to overriding royalties not subject to investor assessments. These augmented investor performance and won much credibility for the company.

When David Higgins met twice annually with Shell New Orleans personnel, he took with him three members of Apache's exploration and engineering staff. The Gulf is predominantly a geophysics play and the information is closely guarded. By fostering the conversation between the two companies, operational relationships and mutual respect grew between the guppy Apache of the early 1980s and big fish Shell.

Ultimately Shell made the decision to vacate the shallow waters of the Gulf in favor of larger oil and gas targets at between 15,000 and 25,000 feet. A number of our oil competitors made their picks in the very high-cost, high-risk deep water drilling, while others still reel from much higher drilling costs at depths of 5,000 to 10,000 feet below the earth, with thousands of feet of pipe in the water before drilling toward the target. This can readily consume a million dollars a day.

In summary, we learned a lot about the Gulf and capitalized on it. Under Jon Jeppesen's leadership as vice president of our Gulf Coast region, Apache began to generate so much cash in excess of capital costs that we had a source of internally generated funds to invest in longer-lived west Texas and deep Anadarko Basin wells, as well as internationally.

THE SHELL ACQUISITION

APACHE'S PARTNERSHIP WITH SHELL WAS successful and led Apache to stockpile cash from its Gulf drilling. We needed to parlay this into a stronger position. I asked an Apache director, whom I knew had done business with Shell in relation to Pennzoil, to request a meeting for Steve Farris and me with Jack Little, the American overseeing the Western Hemisphere for Shell. Mr. Little, no doubt to save his valuable time, assigned an assistant, Paul, to meet and talk with us prior to his own appearance.

Paul explained that, yes, from time to time they would have properties in the shallow Gulf on which we would be cleared to bid. That not being what we had in mind, I twiddled my fingers while Paul and Steve occupied the interlude with pleasantries. About half an hour passed before Mr. Little hastened into the room and seated himself at the head of the table. At that point I started to explain our interest, but he interrupted to note that he was tired of wasting his time on smaller independents, the last one he'd dealt with having defaulted on his payments. To me, the tone was more condescending than cordial. I brought

261

our ten-minute meeting to its conclusion, noting that I was sorry he hadn't had enough time to distinguish between a responsible independent and one of lesser quality, and rose from my chair. Steve and I shared the observation en route to the elevator, "That was a waste of time. We'll have to wait a while." I reported to our director we had run aground and would have to let time pass.

We did not have to wait long. Shell's very able offshore honcho Bob Howard had retired, leaving two senior positions to fill. Royal Dutch Shell's HQ in The Hague sent Walter van de Vijver to the United States to move Shell more rapidly toward its strategic goals, and we picked up on that intelligence before we first met.

We met on a lower floor of the Shell building, and Walter arrived from upstairs within a few minutes of his secretary's alert. Paul shared that Shell had altered its position somewhat, which should please us: Shell would henceforth package certain assets and invite certain of the larger independents to indicate whether they would like to bid, selecting perhaps five independents to bid. "Make that four," I commented, "as Apache will not be among the five."

The remark nettled Paul but not Walter, who noted to us that Paul had recently been promoted by The Hague to head deepwater technology. Paul decided that he could leave and did so. Steve talked on, noting that Apache's people had most of our production on real-time records, which enabled people in need of data relating to their area of responsibilities to access daily relevant figures, and access to these was worldwide. Walter was impressed by that remark, noting he'd like to come over to our office for an in-depth briefing. To determine which conference room to use, I asked Walter how many from his staff he would be bringing. Walter indicating he'd likely be coming alone and a date was set for his visit.

We met at five p.m. of the given day. Apache presenters in our boardroom were prepared and Walter was impressed. Within days, a date had been set for a weekend meeting—a precaution against leaks from either side, despite the strict confidentiality agreement. Walter noted that he preferred a large sale of assets but wanted to give the regional people time to develop an alternative plan to retain and operate selected properties. He had taken production platforms linked to deep-water oil discoveries off the table and the assets to be sold would likely comprise a majority of the shallow-water assets, including all those in which Apache already held an interest and thereby was highly familiar. To the subsequent due diligence meeting in New Orleans, Apache sent seventy people to different hotels on different flights and our then single jet. The deal was sealed soon afterward after Walter noted natural gas prices had begun their cyclical upturn and we agreed to add $25 million to the $600 million purchase price.

The announcement of the deal was well received by the investment community, which had grown tired of being told Apache would stop accumulating "dry powder" only "in due time." On announcement day, Farris and Roger Plank were in New York and I appeared as principal speaker at a large Houston regional investment firm luncheon. Our secrecy had been well protected. Our share price exploded; it had been a win-win situation on both sides. Jack Little soon retired and a large party was given in his honor in Houston, where he was well-regarded and which several Apache employees and I attended.

From Houston, Shell and Apache did two more Gulf transactions and all three cows proved good "milkers." Internationally, Shell was interested in acquiring Far East assets of a large Australian natural resource company named Fletcher Challenge. Would we be interested in Fletcher's Canadian assets that didn't appeal to Shell? Of course—and in 2001 we met the sellers' objectives in another negotiated transaction.

In this way we obtained numerous excellent Canadian properties to which we could add value over a period of years, but there was a problem in the form of a contingent hedging risk. Fletcher Challenge had entered into a prior agreement with Enron, which I believed was soon to go down for the count, unable to make good on the hedges on its books. We acted quickly, taking a loss on that position, while also concurrently closing out all our positions. We lost about $16 million on that element, but Apache came out approximately $90 million ahead overall.

Our own hedging policy was generally to use hedges only to lock in the commodity prices we had used in acquisition estimates. Steve Farris had noted that in planning our annual drilling programs, our annual capital expenditures usually generated sufficient new production to come within 10 percent of the reserve estimates used in our plans. Therefore, Apache's board authorized us to hedge up to half the energy reserves we expected to find and convert to production. Interestingly, our finding costs were easier to predict than the wildly fluctuating prices used in our plans. Many of our competitors—mid-size and then large oil and gas companies—used hedging more aggressively, sometimes winning big, but also losing big when overexposed. Over many years we seemed better able to predict the vicious cycles that severely damaged others' viability, a primary added reason being that our debt ratios had been low enough so that lenders to Apache did not call for us to hedge prices to limit our, and their, credit risk in an overleveraged position, for the simple reason Apache was not highly leveraged.

THE OTHER MAJORS

FROM HOUSTON WE HAD YET to complete a significant acquisition either with British Petroleum, which had eaten Amoco, or Exxon Mobil. In both instances, that was soon to change.

It was almost as though British Petroleum had tailored a transaction for Apache to pursue. Approximately half the monetary value was situated in the shallow waters above a 5,000-foot water depth in the Gulf of Mexico, while the other half consisted of BP's venerable field—and the North Sea's largest producer of record—the Forties Field. Combined, these two transactions broke the billion-dollar barrier for Apache.

The Forties Field had contributed a great deal to Britain and Margaret Thatcher. One of five of its monster platforms had been visited by Queen Elizabeth and her daughter Anne upon its opening in 1975. The Forties Field led the parade of discoveries and development that enabled Prime Minister Thatcher to move her country away from stifling socialism toward a revitalized private sector and advancing standard of living. Britain's coal mines had comprised the primary source of domestic heat and electricity for many years, until the mines began to peter out (not before the soot from the millions of small home stoves and factories had turned the great city London a drab, dull brown). North Sea oil and gas finds enabled "The Iron Lady" to change all that, and for some years to reverse much of Labor-driven socialism.

British Petroleum was pleased to agree to purchase our Forties oil under a contract price that protected the prices we had paid in the purchase. As prices advanced from their cyclical low, once again we did not realize the full market value. However, as hoped, prices both increased, and through working over old wells and drilling into newly found oil within the field, our production from Forties increased by approximately 60 percent, for all of which we realized full market prices. The post-Thatcher government "rewarded" producers in the North Sea with a 10 percent tax increase taken out of the revenues generated.

The tax hike was promptly reflected in reduced drilling and employment, and in declining revenues from the North Sea. Despite having considerable gas nearby, Britain has had to increase its purchase of natural gas from the Dutch North Sea and from Russia's Gazprom. On my retirement from Apache, the Brits were paying Russia up to $12 per thousand cubic feet, double the price at which gas moved in west Texas at a similar point.

When a reporter spoke to me by phone in Houston one day in the early '90s, he asked if we did much business with Exxon, to which my response was, "No, not much." His next question was, "Why is that?" My reply circulated quickly through the oil world: "Apparently, they talk only with God." Incoming calls flooded my assistant Irene Lueckemeyer's line, and in turn mine, from near and far, including The Hague, Australia, and China.

Exxon's unapproachability was about to change. Steve Farris developed topside relationships with the company, and within the next few years we exchanged or purchased properties from them that, at the time, did not meet their hurdle standards. Usually these represented limited production and substantial acreage, for example, in Alberta and British Columbia, while their interest was in deeper, unexplored targets along the Gulf Coast and the Gulf of Mexico, on which they did extensive advanced seismic work and analysis.

When an admired friend at Royal Dutch in senior management took the fall for Royal Dutch on the calculation of reserves at the Gorgon Field, Australia's largest undeveloped offshore gas field, I sold my shares of Royal Dutch, paid the tax on the large percentage gain and more than doubled up on Exxon shares, which I believed to be the best along with the largest of the American-driven major oil companies. Subsequent investment performance, conservative in my old age, vindicated the switch and my admiration of those Exxon senior people I've known and respected, and whose company I have enjoyed.

EGYPT

SEVERAL YEARS BEFORE OUR FIRST discovery in Egypt, Apache joined in the initial seismograph exploration phase of an Egyptian concession in its Western Desert known as Qarun—it was encouraging. We went on to the next phase and encountered oil shows before losing the well in the completion phase. Its nearby second test encountered the same zone and was completed, flowing at the initial rate of eleven thousand barrels of oil per day, a significant discovery.

Phoenix Resources, one of our partners, had enjoyed considerable success in the Western Desert and now had a decision to make. They decided that rather than "people up" beyond its consultants or attempt to raise more capital, it would sell out through an exchange for shares—our shares, as it turned out.

Our friends at Amoco initially estimated we had found a field of 35 million barrels of oil. Qarun and its satellite fields have ultimately tripled the estimate, while additional discoveries in Qarun and other concessions have resulted.

Initially we trucked oil. Later, dual pipelines were warranted and constructed as it became economical to pipe the oil to the concentrated large-volume facilities where we had constructed two large tanking facilities.

In the early days of Egypt's oil history, Amoco had developed very large reserves and production in waters along the Nile and Suez Canal, which contributed substantially to Egypt's economic growth. However, the industry had, as was the practice there, drilled relatively few exploration wells at wide intervals and had basically given up—a senior Mobil officer noting to one of our directors that small fields were not its cup of tea.

Apache however felt differently. We sent seismic trucks roaming over the Western Desert. Soon we were dotting the desert with discovery wells, largely the result of two-dimensional seismic rigs extensively thumping away to provide early drilling prospects and drill enough leads, which followed the pattern of one discovery per four exploration wells drilled. While you need additional wells to find oil to produce commercially, there is usually fallout of noncommercial wells before a field is deemed commercial to develop and produce.

Our early discovery ratio was soon to be improved by our country manager's ready application through organization of a team approach. Our Kevin Ikel took to this like a duck to water. Each team included a geologist, a seismologist, a petroleum engineer, and a drilling engineer. These specialists worked closely together with the able support of Mike Bahorich, who headed the seismic programs and functions as we converted from 2-D to 3-D seismic evaluations, disproving then Mobil's superficial evaluations. Finding costs were rapidly reduced, and we added additional large acreage concessions to our inventory.

I had debated Texas oil and gas executive T. Boone Pickens on the PBS television show The MacNeil-Lehrer Report in the early 1980s. It happened that Bijan Mossavar-Rahmani, of Harvard, had tuned in to the brief interchange between Boone and

Bijan Mossavar-Rahmani.

myself, and liking what I said, had invited me to Harvard's Kennedy School of Government to expand the discussion.

Harvard and Repsol had jointly sponsored a series of annual forums attended by world leaders of the oil industry, to which I was invited. Here I first met Oscar Fanjul, Repsol's CEO, who had put Repsol together in Spain and taken it public. Oscar, a good friend of Bijan's, who moderated these conferences and put out an annual book of papers, made a presentation. Bijan and I became fast friends and spent additional time together in Madrid, where Repsol was headquartered. On two occasions Oscar Fanjul, his wife, and their two sons visited my spouse and me at our Wyoming home. I have been a guest at Oscar's home, most recently in March 2011.

From Oscar and several of his senior executives I learned their views on Egypt's Western Desert potential. They believed that apart from the Khalda Ridge, larger reserve targets lay

271

elsewhere. For example, the largest Western Desert fields were located in western Egypt, relatively close to Libya's border. In Libya, a number of large oil fields had been developed and were producing.

Spain did not utilize trade embargos with the same zest as the United States and therefore Repsol had another reason to pursue its interests in Libya. The greatest reason for Repsol to pursue growth elsewhere was to acquire a national oil company. Argentina became the logical candidate and led to the 1999 acquisition of Yacimientos Petroliferos Fiscales (YPF) as the linchpin of Repsol's integrated strategy in Latin and South America. (Oscar also experienced a degree of saddle rash within the bank-dominated Repsol of Spain. Over a hundred of Repsol's senior people who came with the Spanish companies' amalgamation were more highly compensated than Oscar, their CEO.)

The immensity of the YPF acquisition by Repsol provided us with two mutual opportunities in their strategic realignment of assets, both of financial and people resources. First, they would be more open to Apache's owning their unexplored Egyptian concession holdings that, if later developed, would revert back to the Egypt Government Petroleum Company (EGPC). We could and did find a way for all three parties' owners and people to benefit. Repsol would receive cash and lower its costs. Egypt would benefit from a higher level of Apache investments and added jobs for its workforce, coupled with outstanding mainline opportunities available to a knowledgeable experienced operator who knew the merit and applications of technological advance. And Apache would have a substantial new activity.

For several years, Apache held its December board meetings in Cairo, which also enabled directors and spouses the opportunity to participate in the regional Christmas party event. At that particular period, Apache's outstanding geologist and senior manager, Rob Johnston (who reported to Rod Eichler) was responsible for the company role in the Khalda Concession Company and its exploration.

After the speeches, with dancing about to begin for the couples so inclined, I made my way through the long hallway of the Mena House. Rob Johnston and his charming wife, Kathy, walked up to me. Rob, who has had an almost three-decade-long proactive career, came quickly to the point. "While the bureaucracy associated with EGPC is highly frustrating and time consuming, the potential of the Khalda Concession and the adjacent Khalda offset concession is a perfect fit for Apache, and we have gained the respect of the Egyptian Khalda Concession group, to the point of a high level of cooperation and results. I'm pleading for you to focus on buying Repsol out of Egypt."

I replied, "Okay, I'll run up the high-priority flag."

As I walked above the long black hall, and on the car ride back to the Omni Hotel 10 miles away, I gazed at the Great Pyramids, lit up by lights in the desert night, and began to think about the elements of a plan. In 2001, Apache acquired $410 million worth of Repsol assets.

The Repsol purchase also led to a significant stateside benefit. Repsol's $20 billion-plus acquisition of YPF caused it to readjust its financial structure, and that afforded further opportunity for Apache. Apache recognized its chance, and Steve Farris executed with aplomb. We bought up a west Texas and western Oklahoma swath of property, and a half interest in a large field in west Texas.

At a Tulsa regional operations review, Tulsa requested capital expenditures over the remainder of the year to drill an additional twenty-five wells as rapidly as we could do so. (In Oklahoma,

Rob Johnston in Egypt with the camels.

when an acreage owner proposes a well and a partner does not agree to go forward with the drilling, the reluctant partner loses the opportunity. The acreage then goes to the party proposing the well from which the forfeiting party is able to recover money after the primary risk takers have gained the benefit of several times their costs; the forfeited interests can then obtain their share of residual net revenues.)

At our Tulsa meeting, I asked, "If we accelerate drilling and increase the number of rigs required, would we drive up drilling costs?" Our people noted the drillers we used at the time had added rig and people capacity, and were we to need more, they felt the answer would at this point in the cycle be positive. Further, they felt that were we to contract a number of wells in advance, versus two or three at a time, our costs would start coming down more because of the transportation efficiencies

President Hosni Mubarak and I share a laugh.

associated with multiple wells and attendant supply costs.

More discussions led me to ask the following question: "As long as we presently can raise capital with low-cost debt, suppose we plan to drill one hundred wells instead, enough to move the entire company forward?" You could hear a few good people inhale sharply.

I waited, then Farris noted, "Okay, let's shoot for the hundred, and you guys plan for twenty-five to fifty now with specific status reviews at agreed review points."

It worked like a charm. Why do I discuss Tulsa? The oil business specifically and business at large are related and afford common denominators from which to learn.

Our shareholders should and did gain a leg up on becoming the purchaser of Repsol's Egypt holdings. What I brought to that table was twofold—our corporate culture defined as the sum of a company's values, complemented by the excellent country leadership of Kevin Ikel and his able successor upon Kevin's rotation, Rod Eichler (who promptly upon his assignment set about learning Arabic).

What I sought to bring into the exploration fold was a frame of reference for those to be involved in international exploration, as follows: "When we operate across the barriers of language, history, and culture, it is important to understand that those foreign to us are the hosts and we are the guests."

In Apache's instance I came to realize that our future Egyptian potential was to be based upon mutual respect, so a relationship with its president (the favored title of foreign country leaders, where "sovereign" might better apply) would be beneficial.

Before I could meet with President Hosni Mubarak, I needed an appointment and an introduction. Apache's first woman director, Mary Ralph Lowe, went to her friend, the wife of James Baker, a senior leader of the "Papa George Bush" administration. I also appealed to our then ambassador to Egypt, whose response was dismissive: "I have more to do than to introduce company heads to President Mubarak."

Oh? thought I. I wrote a lawyer friend, Bill White, who was undersecretary of energy to Bill Clinton at the time, inquiring, "What has our ambassador to do that is more important than introducing the head of an American company that is Egypt's largest investor, to the president?" That line tickled the fancy of the Clinton administration, and perhaps in concert with Jim Baker's suggestion may have added to Hosni Mubarak's interest. My subsequent fifteen-minute appointment with Mubarak spilled over to an hour-long discussion. The pre-approaches had been worthwhile.

Frankly, I was amazed by the ensuing results from this relationship, which grew and extended beyond my anticipation and continued to do so, both in Cairo, where I met with Mubarak twice a year, and stateside. I first noted the change upon going directly to my room in Cairo's Four Seasons Hotel. As I entered my room, I was greeted by two male attendants turning down my bed. "Mr. Plank," one exclaimed, "we just saw you on the five o'clock evening news together with President Mubarak, coming out of his office and telling the reporters that Apache is an important investor to Egypt and its people!"

Our second contact was in Chicago, where Mubarak and senior Egyptian cabinet members joined us at a dinner put on by Goldman Sachs. Hank Paulson and John Corzine, then joint CEOs of Goldman Sachs, hosted—shortly before Paulson and his wing of Goldman sent Corzine to the sidelines and hence to politics on the left in New Jersey.

The Goldman dinner meeting was in a hotel where another large group function was being held. The Goldman group of hosts and senior people expected to greet President Mubarak at the main entrance to the ballroom, and gathered there. For security reasons I expected him to enter from the rear, where I stood alone. When he walked through "my door," we walked toward and warmly greeted each other, reaching for each other's forearms. My greeting was, "Mr. President, next time we hug." He laughed and repeated, "Next time we hug." I led him to Hank Paulson as the Americans looked on as though befuddled. Seated at the table, Paulson asked each guest to introduce himself. My contribution, as I recall, was, "Plank, Apache Corporation, which finds Egypt a fine place to do business."

During the course of the after-dinner discussion, President Mubarak was seated across the table one seat to my left. Although Mubarak understands English, he usually speaks from a prepared script. But on this occasion he turned frequently to me, asking for comment as the interaction progressed.

Our next meeting was sponsored by the U.S. Chamber of Commerce headquarters in Washington D.C. On his arrival, noting me, we walked directly toward each other, embraced, and kissed on each cheek while the cameras clicked away. Apache later had T-shirts made of us that were difficult to keep in stock. At the much larger Washington affair I made no remarks and floated no questions. Egyptian and U.S. media coverage would more than suffice.

After the first Chicago function I had cocktails with Bill Hutchison, a senior Amoco executive I had come to know when working on the Apache acquisition of Amoco oil and gas properties. I asked Bill whether their CEO, Larry Fuller, was in Chicago. Yes, Fuller had been invited but declined, in favor of working at his desk a few blocks away. Not long thereafter, John Brown, head of British Petroleum, acquired Amoco, a fine American international oil company, moving quickly to dispense with Amoco's senior management.

British Petroleum Anglicized Amoco, gaining an outstanding swath of assets, from Alaska's Prudhoe Bay to the southern tip of Argentina and to Egypt's still-significant oil production along the Nile and Suez Canal. Those two assets in Egypt and Argentina, I was told by Amoco senior personnel, were that company's most profitable worldwide holdings at the time.

The values we built at Apache endure. As recently as January 2012, my Executive Assistant in Houston, the fabulous Deborah Isaacks Koehler, sent me an Apache news release reported by the *Wall Street Journal*.

George Solich, who had started at Apache as a landman and done the preliminary work leading to our Texaco transaction, went on to start his own company, Cordillera Energy Partners.

Apache is buying George's business for $2.8 billion. This time the values represented in the announced pending transaction were derived beginning with the competence of John Black in the mid 1970s. The production and acreage are situated largely in the Anadarko Basin and to the west in Texas. The acreage falls under the Central Region of the U.S. now headed by very able Rob Johnston, the driving force behind obtaining Repsol's Egypt holdings.

The values in the Solich/Apache transaction have been largely derived from horizontal drilling and hydraulic fracturing of reservoirs. President Obama discussed the issue in his most recent State of the Union Address, deferring to the largely uninformed and too-biased Environmental Protection Agency. Had I not been eating a delicious cookie and drinking ice water, methinks I might have puked over the degree to which politics continue to intervene with the energy industry's ability to add jobs and reduce gargantuan federal deficits were our collective government better informed, able, and willing to make better decisions and act on them.

In one of the Egyptian girls' schools we sponsored.

SPRINGBOARD FOR GIRLS EDUCATION

IN CAIRO, SUZANNE MUBARAK, WIFE of the president, had taken it upon herself to advance girls' education and women's rights in Egypt. Our rotation of the able Kevin Ikel and his outstanding wife in Cairo had called the attention of his successor, Rod Eichler, to one facet of Mrs. Mubarak's program: one-room schools for girls.

Studying every page relating to girls' schools, I thought the program worthy of support and acceleration, and I developed a program for Apache involvement, which consisted of the following: Apache would support the program with limited Cairo staffing, reporting through Glen Joyce to Rod Eichler. Egypt's education system would identify locations for two hundred largely rural one-room girls' schools, soon to be named Springboard for Girls Education. There would be two teachers per school, where thirty-five girls ranging in age from six to fourteen would start up the education ladder, the cornerstone to women's advancement toward equality of the sexes.

Recognizing the importance of male support of the girls' learning, community support would manifest itself by the fathers' donating small plots of land suitable for the small schools. Egypt had built one model school that was up and running, and which a group of Apache directors' wives visited during a board meeting interlude in Cairo. When the meeting was completed, the directors also visited the model school. Looking at the bright, soulful faces of the eager little girls, busily working at their table desks, several directors came to me, noting individually that they each wanted to have a school in their family's name. My plan included signage inside each of the schools, reading as follows: "Dedicated to Egyptian girls, with love." Beneath was written the donor family's names.

Glen Joyce had arranged for the Sawiris family, powerful and wealthy, to receive the largely American sponsors' funds, check the builders' billings, and pay the bills. This would enable U.S. contributors to meet IRS tax-deductibility requirements abroad. The Sawiris group, with strong ties to Harvard University, which has a chair in my name (the Raymond Plank Professor of Global Energy Policy), went well beyond the payout of funds and offered its valued assistance in the selection and training of the teachers. When I inquired of the senior Mrs. Sawiris, "How many teachers do you plan to recruit and train?" she replied, "All of them."

Each year, the Sawiris Foundation funds a modest number of outstanding Egyptian, largely male students to attend Harvard for further education. A Harvard development person headed up a worldwide group of women seeking to advance women's rights, so Harvard went to Egypt's one-room schools for girls.

Recognizing that as our fund-raising efforts could fall behind the timing for the payout requirements, I contributed $1.3 million to the endeavor, out of which I offered to match dollar for dollar the payments of our responding Egypt employees, whose wives' participation and interaction would prove invaluable. A number of our people, able to do so, elected to fund a commitment for an entire school with their own resources. To have schools available to sponsors, I reserved naming rights on one hundred schools during the construction phase. We were able to proceed like gangbusters.

In one meeting I attended personally with Mrs. Sawiris—a wonderful person—and her staff, I remember her response, but not what I said leading to her comment, which I found classic. "Mr. Plank, do you think we live in caves?"

"No, Mrs. Sawiris," I replied, "the food and drink and homes you have lavished on two occasions definitely would never permit such a thought to occur to me!" Our meeting was a splendid and timely step forward.

In one sense, Springboard suffered. Ambassador Moushira Khattab had a senior role in Egyptian public education and she proudly wore some forty epaulets of her positions on her considerable résumé, augmenting her recognition while belying her effectiveness. The pace we needed to maintain the level of school openings essential to complete the two hundred schools, with seven thousand girls in training, found her span of control a major handicap. Dina Kohleffel from Houston headquarters, who drove construction, had the short end of the stick poked in her eye. The Houston coordination end was an overstrain. Nonetheless, she did a truly remarkable job in getting the schools built well and operating.

Egypt owned the schools and the sites on which a number of contractors had erected them. The near-genius youthful architect who had established the models left for further schooling in London and married, and his talents were lost to the project.

Apache received much credit within Egypt and beyond, further augmented by Coca-Cola's building schools, and British sources initiating a program similar to ours. Laura Bush, wife of then President George W., visited our schools and extolled the virtues and applicability within Afghanistan. When Greg Mortenson published his book *Three Cups of Tea*, friends in the States sent me some forty copies. Mortenson, a resident of Bozeman, Montana, home of Montana State University, was correct in assuming the basis for girls' education had not been established in Afghanistan, and girls' schools built under U.S. auspices were destroyed as fast as they were built, the women and girls beaten, some killed.

Aware of our work with Springboard for Girls, Karen Kovach-Webb, who runs the Fund for Teachers pre-K–12 sabbatical program, brought three Houston doctors with her to Ucross, Wyoming, one of whom led an initiative to bring medical services to the poor in Latin America, Madagascar, the Far East, South Africa, and Egypt. At the latter, they found that 30 to 40 percent of our lovely little girls and their mothers had worms. We had believed we could and should look to the Egyptian school system to take over hygiene and medical treatment in the Springboard schools. Otherwise, major negative and costly contagious diseases would set in.

Egypt, like any sovereign nation, would resist American intrusion, as Greg Mortenson found in Afghanistan and Pakistan. At the core of helpfulness to poor and underserved nations is the reality that "Help is help only when perceived as such by the parties being helped or acted upon" (Hugh K. Harrison, 1964). A companion thought, inevitably from Hugh, is that change is threatening, and can be introduced by two means, either with the participation of those affected, or by the more powerful. To me, acting outside of those principles has been one of our government's most conspicuous failures, both internationally and domestically.

Yet when the future of little girls is impacted by worms en-

Special friends of mine for more than fifty years, Terry and Donna Johansen in front of their Egyptian girl-friendly school.

tering their system, crawling into their bloodstream and killing them, do we stand idly by?

As far as I hope to get in the stub period of my life, I want to acknowledge and correct for the downside of imposed rather than fostered change. More importantly, I want to seek challenges like these met neither by foreign countries throwing money on the burning coals, nor by the for-profit sector, but rather through the collaboration of the for-profits with priority local government leadership. We made practical progress in 2010, the second year in which Dr. Todd Price visited Egypt, taking with him medical practitioners who performed deworming plus medical services at "our" schools and among local populations. To lessen the risk of a worms infestation, Dr. Price requisitioned shoes for the students and mothers alike: sixteen

Egyptian school girls wearing Crocs.

thousand pairs per year of Crocs, delivered for two consecutive years—an act of great generousity.

A senior development officer of Yale University, Eileen Donohue, met us in Egypt, visited the girls, and introduced me to Margaret Grey, head of Yale's School of Nursing. I contributed $1.5 million to the Yale Nursing School and Margaret Grey agreed to a formal role in the W. T. Close Foundation, the objective of which is to provide Yale School of Nursing personnel with exposure to direct onsite patient care in underserved poor countries.

Some sixty years earlier, while in pilot training in west Texas, I had met one W. T. Close, and we had become friends at Goodfellow Field in Texas. Bill had graduated from St. Paul's at age seventeen, became engaged at seventeen on his first date with his girlfriend, went to Harvard at seventeen, and married at seventeen. He had spent much of his life practicing medicine and working with underserved, poor natives in the Congo. He was appropriated by Congolese dictator Mobutu as his personal physician while continuing to staff and expand his Congo hospital with largely American nurses. He also was chief physician to Mobutu's killer military.

Bill, father of actress Glenn Close, died in his eighties, and daughter Glenn focused her interests on bipolar disorder, which also afflicts my youngest son, Raby. Before our marriage, Raby's mother, Heather, my third wife, proposed the initial concept for the Ucross Artist-in-Residence Program and ran it for several years. Interested in Springboard Schools, she twice spent over a month visiting the girls' schools in Egypt.

We also noted that high-tech equipment provided by the great company Schlumberger to the schools was beyond the comprehension of teachers and girls alike, and either abandoned onsite or went home with the girls.

Darla Farris, Steve Farris's former spouse, made it a practice on each of her trips to Egypt to carry overseas material relevant to the girls and to shop in Cairo for the girls' needs and deliver personally to the schools what she bought . She made sure to spend enough time at the schools to light up the faces of both girls and teachers alike.

In Egypt, several other Apache-related women gave immensely of themselves. Kathy Neal (with three years in Cairo) became a Springboard director, giving personal time and a continuous effort to the Johnston passion to help others, with the full support of her husband, Rob Johnston. Tom Maher and his wife have both done inspirational work for girls in Egypt prior to moving to Perth, Australia, where he took over Apache's Australian leadership. The immensely caring and capable Dalal

Hanno, executive secretary to Rod Eichler, willed a combined girls' and boys' school to be built, staffed, and supervised. It's a standout, as is Ms. Hanno.

I often asked myself and many others, how can any given country and its people advance, if half the population is consigned to breeding and rearing illiterate, uneducated children. Perhaps some of the ten to fifteen thousand girls the schools in Egypt have served will remember Americans as a positive in their lives and Americans as friends. Egypt was a starting base for our work in girls' schools and the advancement of women, while most of the Springboard little girls were the first in their families to read and write.

EGYPT'S C BLOCK

FOR SEVERAL YEARS, ADVANCING EGYPT'S and Apache's win-win interests, our senior operations personnel had been following the lack of activity on the prospective "C Block," on which the government oil company controlled production. Largely depleted at the time, it reverted to EGPC. Our technical people had studied C Block potential and concluded that in addition to the decrepit oil field, other large leases, largely undrilled, were highly prospective for hydrocarbons at multiple levels above and below the earlier commercial production. When Egypt finally put the acreage up for a round of competitive bids, EGPC rejected all of them, and the million acres lay dormant. EGPC resisted offering the acreage for rebid. Apache's lobbying of EGPC's head, Finance Minister Sameh Fahmi, reached a dead-end, and I concluded it was time to go another route.

Fahmi reported to President Mubarak. As Apache's chairman, I had called for a meeting with the president through the new, very able U.S. ambassador, David Welch, with the approval of our friend, Youssef Butros Ghali, the Egyptian finance minister, who had his own EGPC issues with the ministry. Both Fahmi and his first assistant would be present at the meeting, also attended by Steve Farris and Rod Eichler.

President Mubarak, seated at the head of the table, with Butros Ghali on his left and me seated to his right, turned to me and asked, "Mr. Plank, what can we do for you today?" My response was to suggest that Egypt had on its dormant list a large concession block of acreage, which had been the subject of competitive bids that had been declined. Apache was there to make an offer for the C Block outside the normal bidding process—an offer so good for Egypt that they could not refuse: we would pay $100 million dollars to access all of the block and expend an additional $100 million exploring and developing the block, along with reworking and further testing the abandoned wells and testing to depths both above and below the dribbling and largely abandoned production.

President Mubarak then asked Sameh Fahmi what he thought of the idea, and he was at his bootlicking best, noting he'd considered the proposal and thought it excellent. In reality, Fahmi had previously brushed our offer aside. He had to have been offended at our going around him. Turning to Butros Ghali, the president asked whether he saw any hurdles to overcome. Butros Ghali noted that the parliament would need to approve the proposal and that if it met approval at our meeting, he would prepare to go before them to gain their approval, which he was confident would be granted.

Among the other related issues about which President Mubarak asked questions, he asked Sameh Fahmi by what date he thought Apache could proceed with the work, to which the minister responded it should easily be all systems go by March 15 of the next year, four months from our meeting. At that point I suggested that we use June 1 as our kickoff date. Shortly thereafter we adjourned—mission ostensibly accomplished.

June came and went. EGPC had concluded it needed to formally reoffer the block in three parts for public bids, but that we would be awarded the concessions. Believing this to be punishment for going around the balking minister, I did not think it advisable to go back to President Mubarak. We waited for the bid round results to come in. We were not among the announced winners.

Our next step was to check out the winners and their capability to deliver on their commitments. One was from a player too small to perform; one was a former Russian company, the head of which was on the U.S. senior list of most wanted criminals; and the third was a small "group of businessmen" who wanted to invest in Egypt's Western Desert (which meant to me that they were straw men related to kickbacks to someone). I called Butros Ghali, and gave him the rundown, noting I failed to see how the selection could in any way benefit Egypt. Serious oil companies might already be throwing up their hands in disgust. Butros Ghali said he thought the result could be overturned, with Apache still likely to be able to gain access to the properties.

At his point, I indicated that I wanted to discuss the matter further with Steve Farris and Rod Eichler, for at that time I wondered if the merchandise was not damaged beyond repair.

As has been my practice for many years, I took the dilemma to my Houston apartment that night to cogitate. The first thought I would share with Farris and Eichler was that Apache promptly withdraw from any further interest in the C Block. I believed that we could perhaps make wine out of rotten grapes by coming up with an alternative to the C Block proposal from which Egypt and Apache could both derive greater benefit.

My next priority was to provide an alternative that would deal with the horrible delays of multiple approval levels. Once commercial production had been declared from a new field by Apache and agreed to at the EGPC level, Egypt assigned the production to a concession company, or established a new one to approve, quibble over, or alter each Apache proposal. For example, the Khalda and the Qarun concessions each had concession companies to intermediate plans and engage in necessary field work.

Apache had a group of professionals assigned to the Khalda concession company to work with its managerial staff and ultimately its field hands, as necessary for implementation. When the Khalda production company's approval had been attained, it went to the petroleum minister, and his staff fondled the proposal. It is at the EGPC level, as well as with the Egyptian Khalda chairman, that Apache headquarters senior Egypt staff work on a running basis—however awkward the decades-old process.

My thought on the C Block alternatives was that we reduce the stifling bureaucracy by attaining approval of the plan annually in advance. By cutting through the bureaucracy, the enhanced level of activity would help Egypt Western Desert production and oil revenues grow faster and Apache shareholders to see lower costs and higher morale as the bureaucracy diminished and production and incentives turned from frustration to motivation.

The second night I worked on the new concept, I began to ask myself whether Apache had enough prospective acreage under our control, and more important, what lands we would need back—lands we had been required to turn over to EGPC under the original exploration agreements—so that Apache could double our production in Egypt.

Steve Farris and Rod Eichler liked the concept and Rod's staff began to study which surrendered acreage we needed back. We already had a significant base of three-dimensional seismic assessments, and had drilled, completed, and enhanced production on nearby fields. Several weeks were required to determine the potential, the availability of drilling rigs, and services availability from such companies as Halliburton and Schlumberger, as well as to cost out the plan and prepare to present it.

I smiled to myself. If an approach to the bureaucracy along the way didn't fly, I was confident of two things: First, Youssef Butros Ghali would be able to persuade the parliament to return our once-held acreage. Second, President Mubarak would ensure its approval, overruling any derailment by his petroleum minister. On a number of occasions over the years, President Mubarak had told me of his concern that the formerly major oil reserves produced by Amoco (later BP) had passed peak production and reached a rate of decline threatening to the rapidly increasing Egypt population. We were to have his support in finding new sources in Egypt's giant Western Desert for exploration, discovery, and development of production to mitigate the decline and improve living standards in Egypt's vast, under-explored desert to the west.

True to his word, he and his supportive cabinet, many of whom had been educated in the United States, together followed our discoveries closely.

I had not gone back to President Mubarak to complain when the C Block was awarded to others; rather, I had set about developing a new approach and plan that would be superior to the earlier desired development of the C Block. That plan, pursued internally and by EGPC, worked, enabling both simplification and increased efficiency. Our Egypt production accelerated.

By the time my retirement was in transition, the C Block deal constituted the basis for the biggest contribution to the "Egypt Cause" in my latter Apache years, rivaled only by the Repsol Egypt purchase advocated by Rob Johnston. At that time, in July 2008, the estimated shareholder value had spurted to $15

"Oilmen are soldiers working for the interest of the people," said Hosni Mubarak during his onsite inspection of the Qarun field discovery.

billion of Apache's $50 billion valuation at the point of the Plank-predicted price cyclical meltdown. Production increases and attendant profits, through the excellent follow-up by Egyptians and the commitment by Apache, were well on the way to doubling, while strong oil prices spurred Egyptian employment and revenues.

To me, President Mubarak has been an outstanding leader with courage, capacity, intellect, compassion, and a sense of humor. In my roughly fifty visits to Egypt, I witnessed much progress within Cairo's infrastructure thanks to its diligent and hardworking people. By early 2011, however, amidst the "Arab Spring," my concern for Egypt, Apache's presence there, and little girls learning to read and write stood on shaky ground. Even given the present uncertainties, I'm very pleased that Apache's successful era in Egypt occurred. Egyptians are a friendly and hardworking people to whom education is very important.

FURTHER AFIELD

AUSTRALIA

As Bijan Mossavar-Rahmani crisscrossed the globe in search of waters in which we could cast our production net, a coincidence attracted our attention to the offshore waters of Australia's Carnarvon Basin, in the northwest part of the country.

I received a phone call from Apache's helpful director Eugene Fiedorek, who told me that Hugh Morgan, CEO of Western Mining Company, was interested in Western becoming an Apache shareholder. Western's mining processes had led that company to drill long laterals from a central mining core. This procedure had increased Western's mineral and, under specific conditions, oil production. This was well before the practice of horizontal drilling had become standard across the industry. Anticipating rising oil prices, Morgan wished to expand his company's operations beyond Australia. I told Hugh we'd be pleased to have Western as a shareholder, but asked him to respect our objective to remain and grow Apache as an independent entity. Hugh agreed and honored my request throughout our relationship, which grew over a number of years.

Apache thereby established its Far East/Australian presence. Western sold us an interest in production and also considerable offshore acreage comprising an adequate foothold to justify putting Apache staff on the ground to do three-dimensional seismic work and exploratory drilling. Production growth soon followed, and we expanded our presence through a series of relatively modest production purchases that also served to increase the activity level in the Carnarvon Basin by the industry as a whole.

The "rocks were very friendly," being highly permeable and porous, and we were off to the races. Mobil drilled a fine discovery in which we held an interest, and seeking a field to rival the major finds of the Gorgon and Rankin Fields, stepped out a number of miles and drilled a dry long appraisal well, discouraging to Mobil but encouraging to Apache's geophysicists. We took over Mobil's acreage and promptly added a series of discoveries sizeable enough to warrant a second pipeline infrastructure from Varanus Island, a significant base for storage and treatment facilities. This find and pipeline connected us to growth markets among gold mines and population centers, including Perth, in which we had located our country headquarters under the able direction of John Crum, whose Apache career sprouted wings.

Hugh Morgan was a frequent visitor to Denver, from which he fanned out to visit Western's mining operations in the west. Jackson was a quick jet flight for me from Sheridan, Wyoming, and Morgan and I met several times a year in Denver and Jackson Hole.

Australia is a beautiful country, its distance from Sydney in the east to Perth in the west approximately the span from San Francisco to New York City. Western's Melbourne headquarters, where I enjoyed annual dinners, completed with them the yearly travel route between the States and "down under." Australia's fine wine country lies generally to the north of Melbourne, and dinners at the Morgans' were enhanced by fine reds. From an American business perspective, the fact that the people speak English is a positive. But the climate and environment are so extraordinary that our largely Australian workforce is prone to mere eight-hour workdays, with larger portions of their lives spent out of doors than we find in the States or Northwest Canada.

Variances in resource markets in world areas have much to do with profitability in the oil and gas business. Japan, for example, which grew to be a major manufacturer and exporter in the post–World War II decades, possessed limited coal resources, and essentially no oil or natural gas. So when a consortium of major U.S. oil companies found substantial deep-water natural gas deposits in the Carnarvon Basin, they also developed on-shore facilities on the coast of northwestern Australia to process large amounts of gas into liquid natural gas (LNG). Huge quantities of LNG were shipped on specially-constructed tankers to Japan, Taiwan, and South Korea, where industry and employment thrived. Long-term supply contracts provided good profit margins to the international energy companies, which because of the capacity sold, were less interested in the smaller western coastal Australian markets largely served by smaller companies such as Apache, at then quite low gas prices.

Apache, partners, and competitors initially concentrated on finding oil, and the economics were based on simple arithmetic. It normally requires approximately 6,000 cubic feet of natural gas to equate to a barrel of oil in energy BTUs. At the prevailing price of $3.00 per barrel of oil, 1,000 cubic feet of natural gas was worth 50 cents. Given the large populations of India and China, Far East oil sold at a premium to the benchmark West

Texas Intermediate-(WTI) or Brent-based European crude markets. In Far Eastern oil markets, oil generally brought approximately a $1.50 per barrel premium to WTI or Brent-based crude oil.

When Apache found natural gas in the Carnarvon Basin, the wells frequently flowed ten to fifty barrels of oil condensate per million cubic feet, and Apache's large discovery at East Spar made fifty barrels per million of the high-gravity condensate. When we were producing 50 million cubic feet of gas per day and flowing 500 or more barrels of condensate, a number of our wells were generating very substantial revenues. By reinjecting the gas into a formation, as continues to be done in Alaska's Prudhoe Bay, we were storing the gas until prices made pipeline and onshore facilities viable. Gas markets began to improve with increased economic activity in Western Australia, increasing ten-fold to $5.00 and more per thousand cubic feet. Gas prices equivalent of $30 per barrel indicated a greatly improved market. As gas prices rose, our Australian revenues soared, and the growing profitability was recognized in Apache's stock price, rising with profitability. This enabled larger capital expenditure drilling budgets, which accelerated our oil and gas finding. One discovery suggested possible reserves of several trillion cubic feet, along with a number of less sizeable but profitable reserves.

We found that while we were helping to advance the economy of Australia, Western Australian premiers began to make appointments to visit us in Houston.

POLAND

Geologically, Apache believed that Poland had substantial natural gas. I retain in my Wyoming home great pictures I bought

With Polish Prime Minister Jerzy Buzek in Apache regalia.

in Poland that remind me of our first (and only) significant gas discovery in that country, having obtained them in a shop in Kraków's central square. One was *Portrait of a Nobleman*, and the other a large print of Winston Churchill on the left with cigar, FDR at center, with his saxophone, and Joseph Stalin in uniform under his gray army cap, over the caption, "Never Ending Story."

I was favorably impressed with the oncoming generation of younger Poles in our Warsaw offices, and wherever we traveled within Poland, we found the people friendly, industrious and well educated—a fine match with our U.S. Apache employees.

When the then Polish Prime Minister, Jerzy Buzek, came to Houston, Apache sponsored him and his modest entourage at a large gathering with members of the Business Council for International Understanding at which I was master of ceremonies. Perhaps five hundred-plus attended. The prime minister addressed his audience in English and answered questions warmly and effectively. I presented him with an Apache headdress and a long, clay peace pipe, and we danced a jig. The event had been planned by Apache's very able Tony Lentini.

The dinner, sponsored and paid for by Enron, was held at the city's most prestigious venue, the River Oaks Country Club. Tony Lentini had done his usual splendid arrangements and planning very well. Prime Minister Buzek sat to my left and beyond him was Rebecca Mark, head of Enron's international forays into the natural gas business in Poland, more notably in India, and the water utility businesses in England and Argentina. Fast-talking Rebecca and I had first met earlier that evening, she having arrived on her motorcycle. In the hall she called to me, "Ray, I have to introduce the PM and haven't a clue on what to say." My comment was something like, "I'm sure you can wing it and be brief. He's talented, accustomed to being before an audience and can handle the rest."

During this period, domestic participants in Poland's market came to Apache anxious to purchase gas, locate facilities near our discovery, and pay a favorable price for the gas. While Poland would allow us to negotiate the selling price of our commodity, energy ministers turned over rapidly, leaving Apache with a succession of new authorities with whom to become acquainted. Each of these hospitable leaders was encouraging, but no doubt all were under direction from above to retain control of the price Poland would charge us to transport gas, which rendered Apache without a chance of determining net cash flow and profit potential and estimated risk-to-reward.

As Apache itself rotated bright young engineers into Poland, they were also optimistic that given enough time they would be able to resolve the problems and celebrate an agreement. Despite their commercial logic, we were stymied. Also, we had yet to centralize the company's gas commodity authority and gas marketing function within Apache.

Despite drilling a number of prospects, we had struck out on additional commercial discoveries while adding to our growing costs. Why expose ourselves to a long-term supply contract before agreeing to a quantity and price we would pay to transport the gas? Having seen too many companies that had accepted similar risks collapse in failure for like reasons, we elected to withdraw from Poland and accept a $100 million loss. Because across the company as a whole we had our ducks in order and good places and people to invest, these rationalizations were acceptable.

While we eventually bit our corporate lip, we took one of the half-dozen highly intelligent, motivated, and competent Polish Apache office personnel, Karolina Sokolnik Grabiec, with us to the States. As Apache's plane usually had space for one or two extra passengers, Karolina saw and experienced the Apache world. She has great respect for the company's culture, continues to remain in close contact, and has an intelligent slant on Europe for which her background of fluency in four languages commends her to a fine future.

With my youngest son Raby in the mid 90s.
Today, a fine young artist.

SHALLOW WATERS IN CHINA, 1994—2006

PRIOR TO INVESTING FUNDS AND people in China, Bijan Mossavar-Rahmani and I had adapted our approach to international exploration. Previously, we entered a foreign country by participation in another company's exploration activity. We had in effect, "been there, done that"—had drilled some dry holes, noncommercial discoveries, and made several finds we believed had potential.

As we progressed up the learning curve, though, we changed our approach. While still needing an event, such as a purchase or discovery, to provide entrée, we wanted enough production in a country to be able to provide sufficient cash flow to carry our business operation costs. Under the revised approach it was important to program our strategy as a company that had decided to invest, grow, and become a responsible foreign operator prepared to build, remain, and work with governments for mutual benefit, versus drilling in various oil and gas tracts on a deal-by-deal basis. We wanted to capitalize on our skill sets developed at home and in Canada, and to utilize them more widely.

It became of increasing importance, then, that we consider China far more thoroughly before investing there. There were numerous factors to be considered. China at the time was producing enough oil to meet its domestic requirements. However, its production requirements were rising more rapidly than its aggregate standard of living. The Chinese understood clearly what American leaders including politicians had been oblivious to for fifty years—if you can produce something domestically, and at competitive costs, you don't have to buy it abroad. China could employ more of its then billion people, which spelled more jobs at higher compensation. Several hundred million Chinese were then earning a dollar or less per day.

In China, big, old oil fields were in decline, a condition needing to be reversed. New fields had to be found, and imports increased, for the largest mass of people of the world to move forward. China had gambled on a major investment in its primary energy resource—coal. With peasants moving from the country to major cities, the coal component was generating so much air pollution that, as in politically corrupt Mexico, pollution was inhibiting both vision and health. If Apache could work with the conflicting government companies in China, we could bring our skill sets to bear to mutual benefit.

Texaco had contracted with the dominant onshore company, China National Oil Company (CNOC), to reverse declining production onshore in a major undertaking, while its counterpart, China National Offshore Oil Company (CNOOC), was responsible for offshore exploration and production.

Apache director Gene Fiedorek was very helpful with respect to Australia and China. Gene had formerly been in charge of energy at Apache's then-primary U.S. bank, Republic National

Gene Fiedorek.

Bank of Dallas. He was an admirable petroleum engineer with
international oil company experience prior to heading Republic's energy sector. Republic envisioned a great future in the oil
and gas business.

Gene and Republic's chief executive officer, Charlie Pistor,
thoroughly enjoyed quail and game bird shooting, Gene spon-
soring annual quail shoots in Georgia and pheasant hunting in
North Dakota. I was an annual guest at the shoots and formed
a number of long-term friendships and business relationships
within our industry that proved of outstanding value to Apache.

Early in Apache's history, the board had accepted my proposal that to avoid conflicts of interest no banker, investment
banker, or practicing lawyer, should be appointed to serve on
the company's board of directors. If they had retired, fine—and
if in retirement they gave legal advice, as did John Kocur, fine.
If active in their profession, however, that could create conflicts
and deter us from having true independence. Apache was pru-
dent to waive this stricture with respect to Gene Fiedorek and

with respect to another outstanding director, Joe Rice, a former New York banking CEO whose bank had been knocked off in a hostile takeover. The contribution from their North American and global banking expertise was invaluable to Apache's development, as well as that of my son and current Apache executive, Roger Plank.

With respect to our entrée into China's Bohai Bay, the geological and technical risks were many—yet not insurmountable. Oil fields onshore were proximate and potentially multizoned. Shallow water proved a technical challenge met quickly by our geophysical group, headed by the able Mike Bahorich, now Apache's Chief Technology Officer. Apache rebuilt an old Chinese vessel able to move in shallow water and designed the system by which the geophysical components could be towed behind it, enabling us to obtain outstanding three-dimensional seismic imagery. The Chinese were so proud of this innovation that soon there were look-alikes plowing all over the shallow Bohai Bay waters, closer to shore than conventional three-dimensional devices could go.

Because Bohai Bay was relatively far north among China's oil fields—the closest major city is Beijing—we had anticipated freezing and ice-related production and transportation problems to cause seasonal delays. There were delays, but the ice was also in the Chinese politicos' veins.

We had made perhaps a half-dozen likely commercial discoveries prior to drilling a well at deeper-water depths in our concession. Chinese media proudly proclaimed the Apache discovery to be the largest in China's oil history—fifteen thousand barrels per day. It started the equivalent of a gold rush—but the gold rush was between the China companies CNOOC and

CNPC (China National Petroleum Corporation). Apache was advised of a territorial dispute between the two companies and of further delays before the dispute could be resolved and production begun.

The dispute served China's interests, though not with respect to the well itself. Rather, it gave CNOOC time to move close to our discovery and drill a number of wells into the reservoir on our concession. To me, that was a tremendous heist.

As I considered the series of problems with our China venture, I began to wonder whether China wanted Apache there in the first place, possibly because the government might have preferred to develop the assets itself and had not liked the pressure to which their government had been exposed by U.S. policies before Gene Fiedorek and his number two gained access to the acreage. However, although we tried to trace what had happened before the blocks were awarded, we were unsuccessful.

From Minnesota days I knew well a friend who, with his family, had invested in Chinese ventures on the mainland, and had been well pleased. Another positive was that George H. W. Bush had at one point headed the CIA, and I had come to know him slightly and regarded him favorably. His older brother, Prescott, had promoted investments in China based upon brother George's stint in China.

To gain insights on how to move forward with producing our China discoveries, I had gone to George's retired, close presidential adviser, Brent Scowcroft, asking him to advise Apache at the fee of $30,000 per month. Unfortunately, the information he provided had already been obtained in greater depth by Goldman Sachs, which has closer relations with the relevant sources than did Brent's staff. We agreed to terminate the relationship after three months, as I recall.

Next, we sent our general counsel, Zurab "Koby" Kobiash-vili, a close relative of the U.S. Army chief of staff, to negotiate with China's senior representative, a Mr. Zeng, with whom we had dialogued for several years. We were assured that we were within sixty days of being able to get production under way. Based upon Zeng's promises, we requested that Texaco farm out acreage to us adjacent to our Bohai block, for seismic work to be done and a well to be drilled. The seismic results were positive but China stalled beyond the date agreed. In Houston, we decided that although we had performed the seismic work, the runaround delays not having changed, Steve Farris would notify Texaco's global VP of exploration, a woman who had been helpful in other interactions with Texaco in the normal course of business. First her office reported she was on a brief vacation, then that her husband was seriously ill and she, as the senior authority, was on leave of absence. This delay could make it difficult for Texaco to find a drilling partner in the primary term of its lease from China. I suggested that Steve write to Texaco to formally advise of our withdrawal. Perhaps he forgot, but in any event the Texaco senior next in command was furious and began legal action against Apache.

Joe Jamail, my friend and personal pro bono attorney, had earlier won the judgment that bankrupted Texaco, which wound up in Chevron's hands in 2001. When we approached Chevron, we were told Texaco had a good case and would pursue its claim against Apache. Texaco did so in an arbitration proceeding and to the surprise of both internal and external Apache counsel, who thought we had won the case, we lost. The award was around $35 million—interest, however raised the charge to over $100 million. After the fact, we asked the former head of Texaco exploration and production what she thought a fair pretrial settlement should have been. The answer: $5 million.

Two developments in the interim had favored Apache, had we been able to move from arbitration to litigation. Adjacent to the southwestern concession limits, China had made a commercial oil discovery. Our seismic work had showed that the Chinese discovery extended on to our block, reducing Texaco's risk had Texaco drilled it. The proximity of the discovery to Texaco's block was thereby encouraging to us that should that company negotiate, instead of litigate, the dispute could and should readily have been settled. Texaco may have preferred to win both ways, having by then become Chevron Texaco.

The other positive developed when Mr. Zeng, with an entourage of four or five Chinese, flew to Houston for a Sunday afternoon meeting in an Apache conference room.

In the interim, the Trust Company of the West had become an investor in our concession's overriding royalty in which it purchased interests as they became available. The company's specific interest in Bohai Bay has been assigned by its CEO, Mr. Day, to a senior assistant with whom I had spoken on a number of occasions, and who of course wanted our block to go into production.

I joined the Sunday afternoon session a half hour late on purpose, to allow the group time to get its new proposals on the table. The Trust Company of the West had sent a senior law partner from a respected California firm to attend, observe, and if he chose, to question.

Mr. Zeng stated the Chinese position, which was that they desired a further six-month delay to resolve certain items. When I advised him that they were already two years behind schedule and had been draining our large discovery by drilling into the same reservoir, he began to cough heavily and ask for water. When an Apache employee rose to accommodate him from water directly behind Mr. Zeng on the Chinese side of the table, I noted, "Let them get the water." I wanted Mr. Zeng to understand a new day had dawned.

Mr. Zeng, on recovering his composure, in perfect English pleaded, "Trust me, it will be approved by my government as I have proposed." My response was curt: "Mr. Zeng, 'trust me' is perhaps the most absurd request you could have made! Check tonight and let Apache know at your morning session if you are finally prepared to move forward."

We had determined that we could sue a Chinese-owned company in the United States, and were gambling that little Apache up against sovereign China would find China unwilling to try that lawsuit and impact the bigger picture between the countries. We were prepared to serve papers on Mr. Zeng the following day.

When I rose to leave, so did everyone else. The Trust Company's outside counsel was furious with me, stating he planned to recommend his client litigate against Apache. My response, heard by all, maintained the firm position: "Please feel free to be our guest! You, sir, are obstructing resolution long overdue." Mr. Zeng continued to plead for time. He was personally served papers on the following day. Within forty-eight hours, China agreed to go forward. My Trust Company contact was enthusiastically complimentary in his warm phone call.

Production went forward with full Chinese cooperation. When Apache sent our Chinese partner authorization for expenditures, the Chinese paid promptly. Production accelerated sharply, finally enabling rapid cost recovery. Unfortunately CNOOC had meanwhile drained oil from Apache's largest discovery in the long interval. They had had several straws in our soda.

Problems remained. Under our farm-out agreement with the

Chinese, when we had recovered our costs, we were to turn over field operations to the Chinese. This meant they would be calling the tune and we would be dancing to their music. Under those conditions we would be unable to utilize our capability to add value to the operations of the assets we had developed. We determined to find a purchaser who needed the Chinese to operate.

We found such a purchaser, who paid us a price favorable enough to recover our Chevron Texaco verdict. Since we had been expensing interest charges on our records, upon the sale and closing out the litigation, we reported the recovery of previously expensed costs as revenues in the period, reporting a combined profit—from the oil fields found and from expensive lessons learned. I personally have not purchased a gallon of Chevron gasoline or quart of oil over the intervening years, a minute satisfaction for a very onerous, time-consuming lesson.

Although we entered China for good reasons, in hindsight I neither blame the Chinese nor hold them in contempt for acting in what they were convinced was their country's interest. Integrity is another matter.

SUCCESSION

BY THE TIME I HAD reached my early fifties, I had begun the practice of looking through a wide angle lens for potential successors to my corporate leadership. My criteria were several.

Apache felt it important that we grow and prepare my successor from within the ranks, finding someone of suitable and related background to hold on to the culture and values that Apache represented. In our pre-Apache days Plank and Somekawa had developed and held dear longer-term objectives, including "building to last." The most important of these values was integrity in attracting outstanding professionals and their families who would ensure that we would continue to shepherd the company toward responsible, committed objectives of profitable growth. While Apache's capacity as a leading investor program oil and gas company was preeminent, our building blocks had been numerous and diverse. They were also confusing, both internally and within the investment world of analysts and institutions alike, for whom growth was not enough.

Here let me recognize the influence of Ken Dayton on my life. We had been friends throughout Blake school years, at

Yale, and as we drove together on our 1941 tour of the west. Upon our postwar Yale graduation he had gone on to Harvard Business School, and unlike me, knew his career path would be within the Dayton retail store empire, with Dayton Hudson—now Target. Ken was part of the three-generation family leadership of Dayton's, after which the company progressed under nonfamily leadership.

For the Harvard Business Review and other audiences, he espoused a set of leadership premises, the logic of which was persuasive to me. He believed every manager, from departmental level on up, should be training on the job a "junior partner" whom one was grooming to succeed oneself. By this means, the stream of logical continuity could better be served and upward mobility enhanced.

The power of substantial constructive continuum over many decades was seconded by Omaha's Terry Johansen, my longtime broker and close friend who likes investing with hundred-year-old companies that have navigated through numerous management transitions, paying share owners increasing cash dividends and innovating to succeed in the highly competitive marketplace.

John Kocur was a major influence on my and Terry Johansen's careers and advancement. While John and I were business partners, he got me past some of my naïveté and overly trusting nature, arriving on the Apache scene following the Truman Anderson chapter. One of his sayings was, "The two people I completely trust are my wonderful wife, Shirley, and that splendid person I haven't met yet."

John also used to note with a twinkle in his eye that when a subordinate came to him asking how to do his job, he'd reply,

"If I have to teach you how to do this, pretty soon I'll have your job and you may be seeking another one." Delegation is important. So is mentoring, as every good leader knows. It's important to know the difference between mentoring and command control. I leave it to the reader to think this through.

John and I frequently discussed the qualities and experience desirable in successorship, believing an oil and gas background important and that a candidate's business knowledge alone did not foster a long-term fit. Apache's Management and Development Committee concurred, as it did fit with John's personal objective to remain as president while we had one or more candidates ready.

Phil Byers was ably leading our growing but still small company toward becoming a full-fledged independent oil and gas company. Phil had been a geology major at Dartmouth, with an excellent business management background, and again, a strong family devotion and loyalty. Unfortunately, Phil left the company in 1982.

At one point in Apache's development, I considered Jaye Dyer might be a possible successor. Jaye, with an education in oil geology, was an ambitious man with a highly stable family life and growing swath of corporate experience. He was also well liked in the Minneapolis greater community. And most important, he was dedicated to the principles John and I shared in reaching out beyond self to others; hence, he was a logical successor candidate.

But Jaye Dyer disqualified himself through his association with Remi Gits, who like others prior and subsequent have wanted to break Apache into pieces, one housing our diversified businesses, and the other oil and gas, which he contemplated flipping to Jaye. In fairness to Jaye, I'm confident he was not a co-conspirator with Mr. Gits but had shown natural impatience to align his career within his chosen field of exploration and production.

Mick Merelli had departed from his senior executive role of leading an oil and gas subsidiary of a major West Coast utility. That firm, enamored of the oil and gas business, had overpaid for a company to the point where Mick could not perform for the utility: the acquisition would drag down the utility's ongoing performance on Mick's watch. I lunched with Mick at the University Club in downtown Denver and found both Mick's education and career particularly suited our respective needs at the time. Mick joined Apached as president, as John Kocur stepped aside.

When Mick Merelli joined Apache, he brought with him Steve Farris and several other senior people to lead the operations charge and augment the strong capabilities of John Black and Phil Livingston. We had lost my primary geology teacher, John Woncik, who had gone out on his own, as had Ted Bartling, while Bijan Mossavar-Rahmani, having his Apache tenure under his belt, had formed Mondoil Enterprises, his consulting and oil-based company.

I wanted Apache to go international, which was initially a much debated recommendation. Mick Merelli and I did not agree on either natural gas or foreign exploration. Knowing that gas was a North American multiregional play, I wanted the global search for oil to balance the North American focus on gas, and the oil targets, as noted were bigger and better internationally, which proved to be the case and spurted Apache's growth.

Mick's and my discussions were never heated. We went about our business, in the conduct of which Mick performed in superior fashion. Mick and I came to a friendly parting of the ways, and after a year or so, he agreed to head Key Production, a small

With John Kocur and Mick Merelli, 1991.

entity Apache and I had formed to hold and expand the debt-free asset base. Mick's outstanding performance has enabled Key to be an excellent oil investment while Apache has continued its growth to become a very large and thus far successful independent exploration and production company under the leadership of Steve Farris.

THE IMPEDIMENTS of EGO

"MAN DOES NOT LIVE BY bread alone," is a truism for me actualized by the sense of spirituality. Throughout recorded history within a wide range of fallacies, mankind has believed in a presence beyond itself. Where limited, people have invented or discovered it. In prehistoric times before written history, the printing press, and archaeology, the Egyptian pyramids preserved much of that which was on the minds of the Pharaohs and their families. Constructed in Egypt and beyond as monuments to themselves, over a hundred pyramids would be built by slave labor. Should history condemn or applaud? Neither, I conclude, for what they were or represent can be considered by the millions who have visited Egypt, to wonder, perhaps with awe, at what caused the Pharaohs' egos to be so served and to fail to differentiate right from wrong.

In prehistoric times, the psychological patterns of humanity were already well grounded. While I was a member of the Young Presidents' Organization, several of us studied psychology in a weeklong seminar, a subject I pursued directly with three of the course leaders I most respected. I learned also from an Apache director, Hugh Harrison, who also brought outstanding business and psychology-based learning to me and those who chose to pick up on his remarkable breadth of understanding.

Ego, in the Freudian sense is a good asset to build on and lead with. One's own ego, understood, helps one better understand and be helpful in one's relationships with others. Yet an ego out of balance invariably manifests itself in greed, as a destructive force.

Consider an analogy from our family farm back in Minnesota, where along with milk cows we had a flock of sheep. A dog pack began to kill our sheep, and acquiring the taste of blood, continued to do so. This was when I was about sixteen years old. Our wonderful Doberman pinscher, Von, who guarded home and yard, was pressed into service to protect our flock of sheep. He would accompany Chuck Arnao and me to the sheep pasture, and on noticing a dog chasing the sheep, Von would swiftly overtake and kill the marauder. As the other dogs fled, Chuck and I would pick them off with .22 soft-nosed bullets from our Hornet rifles until, after several days, the wild dog pack was no more. My point here concerns "the taste of blood." It exemplifies the negative impact of overdeveloped ego, and greed, which once released within any organization, exposes it to the release of forces that, unchecked, threaten sheep herds and corporations alike.

The case of Enron provides a latter-day example. (A correct assessment of the game Enron was playing five years before its shareholders, including many of its employees, read the signs, both saved and made Apache investors money.)

Greed topped integrity as the mastermind, Ken Lay (not Jeffrey Skilling), led it to self-destruct. When headquartered in Denver, Lay was a respected standout figure. In my opinion, having been born of or into a family where his father was a minister, Ken must have become motivated to make waves, using his PhD in economics and early Washington exposure to provide him a base. He was highly visible in business and charitable work, and in Houston's social circles and political arenas. His progress in the pipeline utility business and in a subsidiary oil and gas exploration company added to his standing. His personality was one of warmth and affability, while internally, well-stated rules and policies went on record.

I liked Ken. We often sat together at business luncheons where in discussion we appeared to be in accord. Not so with his partner: Jeffrey Skilling, quick and braggardly on his feet, was quick also to attack behind my and others' backs. I came to conclude Skilling to be the "hatchet man," while beginning to recognize company actions that on the surface were sold as constructive to the independent oil companies by word, were ruthlessly conflicted by deed. Its financial segment soon reported to Skilling, who was brought forward as a Harvard hot shot, and to McKinsey & Company business consultants.

Investment firms were swift to pursue the massive fees from offerings by Enron and its subsidiaries. Their jet pilots noted to ours that overseas, large company jets were frequently used for hauling furniture and for family purposes that they did not believe could or would be able to continue under scrutiny, and with which they did not wish to be identified.

One Christmas, a friend and I were driving from Ucross, Wyoming, to the home of Annie Proulx, the Pulitzer Prize–winning author who had written portions of two books at the Ucross Foundation Artists in Residence Program and made very helpful contributions to the colony and to Sharon Dynak, now the Ucross Foundation's able president. En route to our Christmas-day dinner with Annie, I finally looked up from having been engrossed in Enron's proxy study to find we had driven 30 miles beyond our turnoff, making us so late we were graciously invited to spend the night with nearby friends after her fine turkey dinner.

It was important to Apache that we understand what Enron was up to, because so many hedges cleared through Enron. On a business trip to Apache's Buenos Aires office, I inquired of an investment banker what he could tell us about Enron's integrity. In carefully chosen words, he noted a person closer to Enron had posed the question of an Enron senior officer, "With [Enron's] stock having backed off from its high in the nineties to thirty-five, it might be a good buy. What do you think it's worth?" The rejoinder was mimed—the officer held up his thumb and middle finger, making a zero. From our plane we called Houston and ordered the liquidation of all hedges—and, our banks granting favorable timing, we made $90 million even after taking a several-million-dollar loss on one hedge by Enron against asset purchases in Canada, where the value of the hedge had been attributed to it in the asset purchase price.

Enron's specific failure derived from selling assets of controlled-related subsidiaries above market value to add to reported earnings. Overpaying for purchases while borrowing against inflated assets, and attributing earnings to distant, long-term hedges that it viewed optimistically, compounded Enron's credit needs until its faulty financial lifeline broke, and hundreds doing business with the company shared the big splash. Having acquired substantial personal wealth, Ken Lay was convicted of fraud in May 2006. He died suddenly less than two months later, before sentencing. That October, Skilling was sentenced

In 2002, I testified about the need for reform in the natural gas market before the Energy and Air Quality Subcommittee of the House Committee on Energy and Commerce.

to twenty-four years in prison.

On concluding that Enron was a perpetrated fraud, I estimated it must be accompanied by a number of sleazy operators in the deregulated pipeline business. I figured they were all Humpty Dumpties which would take a great fall, and for a while considered piling up a great fortune by shorting them. Deciding that was not a means of fortune building I could not in conscience pursue, I did not partake, despite identifying those I deemed culprits.

Japan has had the multicentury practice of disemboweling oneself in hara-kiri, when failure takes the place of achievement. Whether suicide or natural causes may have claimed Ken Lay's life, being a hero in the eyes of the public or in his perceived self-image may have made a prison sentence intolerable. In my view, contrast is one of the spices of life. I did not choose the Enron route.

MY FATHER

PASSION AND COMPASSION

Passion for all endeavors, including business,
education, civil and humanitarian rights.
Passion for land stewardship and the arts.
Passion for high moral standards and integrity.
Passion for life.

Compassion for the individual, be it prince or pauper,
to treat with respect and equality.
To challenge and encourage each individual to become more fulfilled,
and often providing a means to do so.
Compassion for humanity, to create opportunity for those not yet born.
To offer a better life in a better world.

To make a small difference.

-Mike Plank

With my son Mike at the construction site of the Raymond Plank Library and Center for Land Stewardship.

LIFETIME LEARNING AND THE VALUE OF TEACHERS

SOME MAY FEEL THAT WHEN we learn to read and write, we are ready to climb the mountain to our future destiny. My parents' goal for us was a good college education, after which they assumed that at approximately twenty-two years of age their offspring could and should be well enough prepared to choose, grow, and make their own way. Prior to, during, and following the formation of Apache, I have assiduously filled in blanks of knowledge and experience with "lifetime learning."

With the benefit of hindsight, I can now see that, as at Blake in the '30s, while at Yale in the early and mid '40s, I had great teachers who inspired me. Three stand out.

Arnold Wolfers, from Switzerland, Master of Pierson College at Yale, was a great professor of international relations and mentor of FDR's secretary of state, Dean Acheson, who sometimes allowed him access to FDR. While occasionally Arnold Wolfers would "guest lecture" a class, our more direct contact was at lunch in Pierson College's dining room. One evening, when Brooks Fields and I were invited to bridge at the Wolferses' (a great honor for us), Secretary Acheson came to see Dr. Wolfers. He

With Brooks Fields at Yale.

was brusquely turned away by the Wolferses' attendant with the words, "Mr. Wolfers will see you at nine a.m. at the scheduled appointment." The Wolferses preferred to pursue our bridge game!

My second great professor was "Gentleman Jim" Leyburn, who headed the Yale Sociology Department; I both took his course and often rode with him on the train to New York City to stay with my sister, Ruth. Professor Leyburn rendered sociology inspiring.

And my third great professor was William Lyon Phelps. As college freshmen we'd gather at his feet one night a week to listen to him speak on a variety of subjects. We sat on the floor because there were no chairs or tables to lean against—all space was given over to books, many from authors who hoped the great professor might write a foreword or provide a quotation for the cover.

Dr. Phelps had a remarkable capacity to cover several serious but interrelated topics concurrently and yet knit them together at the end. Dr. Phelps was expert in "connecting the dots" into coherent relevance, which I did not recognize at the time later represented a deferred awakening of underscoring analogies. From these lectures my first takeaway became, "Everything is related to everything else." Phelps also demonstrated how to identify with a listener's interests by listening in turn for what was of interest and addressing it rather than launching into a presentation that might otherwise have caused a mind to wander or close in the first two minutes.

When graduating college in 1946, at age twenty-four, after six war-related years, my career objectives were to start a business, become successful in that work, and fill in the gaps necessary by taking short courses and perhaps reading ten thousand books in my lifetime. I wanted to lead a full, happy, and productive life, one motivated to be helpful to others' assuming worthy goals. Better to come down on the side of helping others than lead a self-centered life of unchecked ego and greed.

It did not take long for many of us of similar age, and with perspectives derived from surviving the deadliest war in history, to realize that we were but pulling aside the curtain, in realizing how much we would need to learn over the years ahead. I began to comprehend what lay before me with regard to filling certain gaps and also reaching beyond one plateau after another to the elevations above. A distinction I came to appreciate was a preference to reach out less vertically and more laterally to encompass, understand, and be functional in respect to capacity and motivation. In my early business years, it was readily apparent that the capacity of most individuals is far greater than we may assume possible.

For lifetime learning, the requisite tools are those readily at hand. I have found it valuable to remain pragmatic while adding to a growing personal skill set of management tools.

While in the discovery process and experiencing challenges finding and producing oil and gas, mentors such as Apache cofounder Ted Bartling, and superb conceptual and trained geologists such as John Woncik and John Black—all three in Apache's Tulsa office—grounded me in the fundamentals, as did George McLernon's remarkable intelligence and sense of humor in the 1950s and 1960s.

Along with serving on boards of businesses in the Young Presidents' Organization, I identified two tools to self-education that I found most instructive. The first was the *Wall Street Journal*, which I studied closely enough to understand everything printed or charted to identify helpful content. And in my first two offices, on the full-length wall behind my desk, was a peg board on which hung public companies' annual reports with attendant shareholder proxy statements of a variety of firms: those in which I held shares, those owned by a group of mutual funds plus at which I served as a board member, those held by several investment clubs, and those held by not-for-profit charitable investment committees of which I was a member.

I knew I needed to understand in depth the financial side of business; oil and gas taxes, both federal and state; investment banking; and primary regulatory commissions that included the Securities & Exchange Commission, the Internal Revenue Service, and the Federal Energy Regulatory Commission.

I needed to know enough in each of these areas to be able to innovate and lead Apache to be a strong force and competitor within its industry and in the oil program business, where we were to become a leader of the pack.

In looking back on the decades, I'm surprised to realize that what I did not know has been a tremendous advantage, versus a liability. I had not fallen victim to how others learned, knew, and practiced. We were able rapidly to develop the Apache way, and with it a strong corporate culture based on values and the ability to countermand the adage, "Beaten paths are for beaten men."

REFLECTIONS ON SPIRITUALITY

IN THE INTRODUCTION I REFERENCED Dad's words to me as a youngster, "Son, over my life I've found it useful to try to make a very small difference on behalf of others." I've wondered why he emphasized a very small difference. Was it modesty? Possibly. Was it more likely that he was offering a thought less for direction and more for consideration? Certainly he was not sermonizing. What were his expectations of me, if any? He left me with an open field and an open mind—a dictum, not a dictate, God bless his soul. It was up to me to live my life as I so willed. Was there a religious component undergirding Dad's pearls of wisdom? Possibly; both my parents were deeply religious. However one wishes to define spirituality I believe in its relevance.

That which I specifically wish to avoid is to sermonize or to recommend. Dad did not, nor did Mother in her last note to me: "Keep your head up and your courage and faith high." Nor are my beliefs with respect to religion conventional, nor in any way an attempt to influence others.

Spiritual leadership, to my eye, has been far from exemplary. I

In front of our non-demoninational chapel at the Park at Ucross 2012.

found the Christian missionaries sent forth to convert the "heathens" to Christianity too peremptory. And the Spanish brand of Catholic Church, complete with an index of books unsuited for human consumption, was not organized religion's finest hour.

Yet colleges and universities of religious derivation are useful, and most religions serve mankind and so are on the positive side of life's ledger.

In World War II, when I was engaged in the Pacific theater, there were "no atheists in fox holes," or among our crews, as far as I was aware. We prayed for survival and our nondenominational chaplains were among my closer friends. In the Philippines, we crew members helped build our chaplain's chapel.

Like former President George H. W. Bush, who before college became a navy dive bomber pilot, I had enlisted in the U.S. Army Air Corps to become a pilot, idealistically to end wars—

wars in which, whether the enemy be Japanese, Russians, or their vassal states, men and women alike prayed to their gods.

At that time my eldest sister, Ruth, worried that I had in my makeup a subliminal death wish, and I could not persuade her otherwise. I argued that America had stood up for our beliefs for three hundred years and it was my generation's time at bat. How could I turn my back on human freedom and those who had gone before to carry the burdens of serving our nation?

Where then do I, seventy-plus years later, stand on the topic of religion? Do I believe in God? Yes, I do. Do I pray? Daily, though occasionally falling asleep in the act. Do I believe in heaven, hell, and eternal life? Yes and no. With so many conflicting religions in the dangerous contemporary world, I believe in a presence.

Where I locked horns with traditional Christian faith was and is concerning life after death, purgatory, heaven, and hell. And with all the various faiths in play, why not have my very own little brand? While I believe in the characteristics of heaven and hell, I believe in the concept of "heaven on earth" fits the bill, as does "hell on earth" for the rotten apples in mankind's basket.

I am moderately repulsed by the notion of asking for forgiveness on one's deathbed, or to repent and get a golden set of wings and be saved. Too easy: "See no evil, speak no evil," or "The meek shall inherit the earth." Instead of "turning one's other cheek" to psychopaths or sociopaths, for example, of whom I've met a few over the years, I prefer to believe they are likely to experience the penalty box during their lives on earth. On the positive side, when a person seeks to lead a constructive life in behalf of self and others, life can be fuller, more con-

With my father in 1925.

structive, and with soul, closer to "heaven on earth."

In my lifetime there has been room for spirituality, loyalty, and a sense of fair play. I've often wondered about coming through a war unscathed and healthy, after flying so many missions in which death was all around me. Was I just lucky? Or was there a reason why my life was spared because of "a presence?" I choose to believe the latter and in doing so, come down on the side of spirituality. My belief received a significant boost from an Apache scientist-mathematician who had concluded that the Earth was too remarkable, too perfect to have been an accident, but rather must be attributed to a presence—or God—who cared to provide the miracle of energy millions of years earlier the better to serve mankind's needs and life itself.

With my mother in 1930.

My role in this personal history will have been complete in 2012, my ninetieth year, a personal blessing in and of itself. How so? Over the thirty years since taking pen in hand, the experience I have derived from lifetime learning has accelerated from a strong, early base. My rate of mental absorption from reading, global travel, and observation has been greater in the last decade than in prior decades, the fact of which has pleased a number of persons desirous of making a contribution beyond normal retirement age.

To the reader I pass along the final words of my mother: "Keep your courage and faith high;" and of my father: "Try to make a very small difference on behalf of others."

ACKNOWLEDGEMENTS

My inspirational loyalists:

Sharon Dynak
John Gulla
David & Jane Higgins
Deborah & Edward Koehler
Carol Melver
Joyce & Steve Singular
Karen Kovach Webb
The Big 10!